Stop Battling Disease & Start Building Wellness

THE COOKBOOK

Brent & Katie

Great Health from my kitchen to yours—

Toni Jean Kulpinski

Stop Battling Disease & Start Building Wellness

THE COOKBOOK

Your Guide to Extraordinary Meals

Tonijean Kulpinski, CBHC, BCHP, AADP
Board-Certified Holistic Drugless Practitioner

Copyright © 2019 by Tonijean Kulpinski

All rights reserved. No part of this book may be reproduced or transmitted in any form or by any means without written permission of the publisher, except in the case of brief quotations embedded in critical articles and reviews.

This material has been written and published solely for educational purposes. The author and the publisher shall have neither liability nor responsibility to any person or entity with respect to any loss, damage, or injury caused or alleged to be caused directly or indirectly by the information contained in this book.

The author of this book does not dispense medical advice or prescribe the use of any technique as a form of treatment for physical, emotional, or medical problems without the advice of a physician, either directly or indirectly. The intent of the author is only to offer information of a general nature to help the reader in the quest for well-being. In the event the reader uses any of the information in this book for self or others, which is a constitutional right, the author and the publisher assume no responsibility for the actions of the reader.

Statements made in this book have not been evaluated by the Food and Drug Administration. This book and its contents are not intended to diagnose, treat, or cure any infection, injury, or illness, or prevent any disease. Results vary and each person's experience is unique.

Statements made and opinions expressed in this publication are those of the author and do not necessarily reflect the views of the publisher or indicate an endorsement by the publisher.

ISBN: 978-1-945446-60-3

I dedicate this book to my Grandma Frances: not only were you the most loyal and loving grandma I could ever hope for, but you gave me all the skills I needed to become a wonderful cook like you. I know you're looking down upon me as I continue to embark on this journey helping others heal through some of your great dishes. I'll always love you, Grandma. Have the aprons ready until we meet again.

Thank you, Jesus, for blessing me with so much, especially the knowledge and wisdom to create another book so I can bless forward. I do nothing without you, Lord.

To my beautiful daughter Michaela, I love you more than life itself. You are my everything, and I thank you for believing in me so I can believe in myself. You are forever my precious baby girl.

To my beloved husband, Vladimir—you have been my rock, my soulmate, my lover, and my friend. I couldn't do any of this without you. I love you so much, and I look forward to forever with you.

Peanut, you are truly my best friend. You are right by my side through everything. We have shared many wonderful moments together. I am so grateful to still have you in my life through a second book. Thank you for your continued patience when you want my attention. You are above and beyond special to me. Thank you for rescuing me, and I will always love you.

PRAISE FOR
STOP BATTLING DISEASE &
START BUILDING WELLNESS:
THE COOKBOOK

"This eagerly anticipated book is finally here for all to enjoy! Toni's recipes are not only delicious, they will help you heal. Toni shows that eating healthy is not about depriving yourself, in fact it is the complete opposite. It's about abundance and your body will respond with a gleeful hallelujah!"
— Nicole Roberts, client whose lupus was cured under Tonijean's care

"What I love most about *Stop Battling Disease & Start Building Wellness: The Cookbook* is how Tonijean **makes it clear that when you pass down recipes from generation to generation you don't have to pass down the diseases along with them.**"
— Frank Tortorici, Certified Fitness Specialist, Holistic Wellness Coach, and Functional Diagnostic Nutritionist

"Thank goodness for Tonijean Kulpinski's delicious creations on how to stop searching for another diet and just eat real whole foods the way nature intended! She is such a wealth of knowledge on how we can take steps to eat better and live life to the fullest."
— Chris Luppo, Christian Women in Media Association, Northeast Director, TV Management/Producer

"When I have a question regarding my health, the health of my family or even the health of my pets, the first thing I do is go to Tonijean's book, and it always holds the answers for me. Tonijean is an eternal fountain of knowledge for your physical health, spiritual health and emotional health. I am thrilled to see her cookbook finally come to fruition and I am so excited to have all of these recipes right at my ready in my own kitchen! Real food in the form that God created is the medicine that heals, and now we can all benefit by following the delectable recipes in *Stop Battling Disease & Start Building Wellness: The Cookbook*."
— Felicia M. Dopico, Bestselling Author of *Journey Out of Egypt: A Mother's Journal of Her Daughter's Miraculous Survival and Recovery from Traumatic Brain Injury*

"I want to encourage you to try every recipe in this cookbook and lead your family to extraordinary health."

— Bill Lemanski, TV Host, Producer of *Book Talk*,
Freelance Journalist, and Award-Winning Author

"After reading Tonijean's first book, I am so inspired to incorporate these life-giving recipes in *Stop Battling Disease & Start Building Wellness: The Cookbook*. No one else has ever explained so clearly my body's ability to heal and live disease free."

— Jody Caffaro, Middle School Teacher at Hawk Meadow Montessori School,
BA in Psychology, and an MA in Education Leadership

Contents

Acknowledgments — 11
Introduction — 15

CHAPTER ONE
My Personal Testimony — 19

CHAPTER TWO
What Is Organic Food? — 23

CHAPTER THREE
Eating Organic on a Budget — 25

CHAPTER FOUR
Breaking Your Fast — 31

CHAPTER FIVE
Breakfast — 33

CHAPTER SIX
Soups — 47

CHAPTER SEVEN
Salads — 59

CHAPTER EIGHT
Appetizers — 93

CHAPTER NINE
Dinner — 111

CHAPTER TEN
Snacks — 151

CHAPTER ELEVEN
Desserts — 159

CHAPTER TWELVE
  Dining Out and Vacationing   203

CHAPTER THIRTEEN
  Fresh Juices and Smoothies   205

CHAPTER FOURTEEN
  Cooking and Baking Equipment   215

CHAPTER FIFTEEN
  Sample Daily Menu   217

Conclusion   223
Resources   225
Index   231
About the Author   243

Acknowledgments

Mom: I first want to thank you for loving me unconditionally. You are the foundation of our family, and you give me exactly what I need to move forward to succeed. I love you, Mom, now and forever.

My dear husband, Vladimir: I want to thank you with all my heart for dedicating so much of your time and patience through your outstanding photography skills. You have made my cookbook such a delicious work of art. I am forever grateful to have built this wonderful memory with you. It has brought me so much joy watching you enjoy the delicious creations. Grandma Fran always said, "To get to a man's heart, you must go through his stomach."

My amazing sister, Francesca: We did it, two best-selling authors, yay! Fran, you are everything I would ever hope for in a sister. I'm so very proud of you for so many reasons. I could never see my life without you. You know exactly what to say when I'm down, and you know just what I need when I'm unsure. Thank you for being the best sister I could ever imagine. I love you with every beat of my heart.

My dear brother, Richard: you have believed in me right from the beginning, and I thank you for the countless hours of lengthy conversations teaching me what would take me straight to success. I love you, my little brother, with all my heart. Keep shining!

My precious niece, Michelle: you are such a gift from God. I am forever blessed to have you as my niece and my friend. Thank you for your words of wisdom and encouragement to continue this journey. I love you more than you can ever imagine.

Christian, Selah, and Elion: you three are the best little nieces and nephews that I could ever ask God for. I love you all so very much, and I pray a multitude of blessings upon you.

Franca Amato Sanchez: thank you, my precious sister, for all your love and support. I love you now and always.

My amazing friend, Nicole Roberts: I don't even know where to begin because there's so much that you've done for me. I am forever blessed with your amicable friendship. I love you as if you were my sister. *Thank you!*

My dear friend, Angela Wallace: I thank you with all my heart for your incredible friendship, and I look forward to a lifetime with you. Angie, I love you to the moon and back. I pray God's blessings upon you.

Christine Felicello: the only way to describe your friendship to me is to say that you are truly my family. We have been through so much together, and I wouldn't change one moment of it. I love you so much, and I thank you for your ongoing love and support. Christine, I look forward to many more years to come with you right by my side.

Kathy Meroney: *Angel* is always my first thought when I'm thinking of you. You have every aspect of a true-life angel. You, Fran, and I go way back; our journeys reflect in my thoughts like a movie. We've had great times and difficult times, but because of our strong, Godly friendship we not only got through them, we got the victory. Your friendship is like no other, and I love you like my own family.

Oh, Lennis Giansante Lubrano: I can't thank you enough for all your constant prayers and for seeing and believing in what God had for my future. I'm so glad I listened to you. I love you so much my dear, precious friend.

Lisa Buldo: thank you for your friendship, prayers, love and support, and for having me on your show. I'm forever blessed. I love you, Lisa.

Felicia and Abigail Dopico: you have always supported me on my path of health and wellness, and I am truly grateful. More importantly, it is a blessing to have your friendship. I thank God for both of you. May He continue to bless you on your new and exciting journey. Love and blessings.

Nancy Pierro: I thank you so much for all your love and support through the years and I look forward to a lifetime of friendship with you. Love you, my friend.

Keith and Maura Leon: first and foremost, I thank you for everything that you've taught me on this incredible journey. You are two of the kindest and most selfless people I know. I will never forget the day on the phone with Keith when I was having an issue with something, and you were giving me sound advice and in your words, you said to me, "I'm your publisher and your friend, but I'm your friend first." Tears rolled down my face to know that we are all literally a family, a team that has each other's backs. I've truly grown to love you both. I am forever changed by this journey from the very beginning until now. Love and many blessings to you always.

As for everyone else at Babypie Publishing: Karen, Heather, Autumn, Rudy, and Maryna—thank you for all your hard work with Editing, Production, and Layout and Cover Design to bring my manuscript into an incredible book.

Charice Damiani: thank you for your friendship and love. Looking forward to many years with your friendship. Love you.

My beautiful and dear friend, Laura Thompson: you are most definitely my soul sister. From one author to another, I'll love and cherish you forever.

Angela Locker: you and I could probably write a book together and I'm sure it would be a best seller. I can't thank you enough for just, everything. Love you, my friend.

Tammi Boyd: I am so blessed to call you my friend. Thank you for all your encouragement, love, and support. I pray an abundance of blessings upon you and your family. Love you.

Cameron Cushing: I owe you a huge thank you, not only for your beautiful friendship but for leading me to Babypie Publishing. Much love and abundant blessings to you, my dear friend.

Everyone else: I thank you from the bottom of my heart for choosing my books as your nutritional resources and for all your support. I am forever grateful.

Introduction

Welcome back, and congratulations for reading my first book, *Stop Battling Disease & Start Building Wellness: Your Guide to Extraordinary Health*. Now that you're a health expert and understand all the aspects of how to build wellness in your body, let's enjoy some wonderful meals, refreshing beverages, and delicious desserts.

If by chance you have not already read my first book, please purchase your copy on Amazon or Barnes & Noble, as my first book is a necessary resource guide. *Stop Battling Disease & Start Building Wellness: Your Guide to Extraordinary Health* will help you understand all the ingredients used in this book.

In my first book, you learned the importance of consuming food in the forms God created to avoid the toxic overload of chemical crop enhancers. You learned that organic food is the only way nature intended our food. Eating nonorganic food has the potential to not only cause sickness in our bodies but also to pollute the environment. I suggest when you create each recipe from this book, you choose organically sourced ingredients. Choosing organic ingredients can assure you that your meals have optimal nutritional value and superior flavor.

Many of the recipes in this book are revised versions of recipes I learned when I started baking and cooking with my grandma at the age of seven. I took the wisdom of Grandma Frances and my God-given, nutritional knowledge and recreated these recipes. The primary difference is the source of the ingredients—from refined, nonorganic sources, to organic, unrefined, whole-food nutrition.

There is absolutely nothing wrong with food in its original form. Sadly, much of the foods we get in stores and restaurants is treated or raised in ways that harm us. Please allow my book to inspire you to recreate your traditions by simply changing the source of your ingredients. Follow the principles that you have learned in my first book. Passing down recipes from generation to generation should be happy, joyous moments of health-giving memories, not recipes that have the potential to make you sick.

I must make a confession about my family's cooking and baking history. Coming from an Italian family, using exact amounts really wasn't our thing because we would add a little bit of this and a little bit of that. Yet, our creations were perfectly balanced and delicious. With that said, the lack of accurate measurements made it a little difficult to write a cookbook. Sometimes, I couldn't even remember what I had used in a specific recipe and had to carefully recall what I did. Luckily, my passion for cooking and baking led me right back to the ingredients that I use now, and my efforts have been successful.

Food for Thought

Although I choose to be vegetarian, I strongly believe that no matter what dietary choice you make, the source of your ingredients matter. I am not here to convince you to become a vegetarian. My goal is to deliver the message of health and healing through education. My hope is to see you make wise decisions regarding your food sources when choosing a specific diet that is best for you.

Where your food comes from has a major impact on your health. In this book, I made sure I have created recipes for all dietary choices. Whether you choose to be a meat eater, a vegetarian, or a vegan, you will find recipes in this book. I believe that a plant-based diet is one of the best diets to choose; however, following the principles in my first book will guide you in making the best decisions on choosing food sources for yourself and your loved ones.

When someone learns that I'm a vegetarian, the first question they ask me is, "Where do you get your protein from?"

Please allow me to elaborate. The question should not be whether we are getting *enough protein* when not eating meat, but whether we are getting *enough fiber* when not eating enough vegetable and plant-based foods.

Protein is a chain of amino acids that are essential, or necessary, in every living thing. Plants can take nitrogen from the air and convert it into amino acids. Plant-based foods contain protein, carbohydrates, fat, and fiber, which make plant foods a complete meal.

When you consume grass-fed and pasture-raised animal products, you're actually eating recycled, plant-based protein, *minus* the fiber. For example, a meal consisting of broccoli, avocados, and quinoa provides up to 60 grams of protein, which is three times the amount of protein in a 6-ounce slab of beef. Yes, you read that right! So, if you're a vegan or a vegetarian, the next time someone asks you where you get your protein from, you now know exactly what to say.

The modern food industry tells you to consume fruit in only small amounts or simply not at all, typically because fruit contains sugar. This reasoning is wrong. Fresh fruit sugar does not have the same impact on the pancreas as sugar from the sugar bowl. Refined sugar is processed with high heat temperatures and is sometimes bleached or milled, which removes the minerals and nutrients, making it difficult for the pancreas to process.

The average person who consumes the Standard American Diet (SAD) has a spike in blood glucose from eating fruit only if their pancreas is already malfunctioning. Your pancreas is the organ that helps regulate the body's glucose or *blood sugar*. The body runs on sugar or carbohydrates in the form of *polysaccharides*.

Polysaccharides are the carbohydrates that consist of sugar molecules bonded together in the form of starch and cellulose—the cell fibers and walls of all plants.

Low-carbohydrate or no-carbohydrate diets are some of the worst diets you can consume. Now, don't get me wrong, modern grain carbohydrates in the form of refined pasta, bread, bagels, cookies, crackers, muffins, cakes, pastries, and wheat should be completely avoided. In my first book, the chapter entitled, "Don't Go Against the Grain," explains why these carbohydrate sources are detrimental to our health. Fresh fruits, however, are some of the most nutrient dense and mineral rich foods on planet earth. Avoiding them may very well set the stage for failure of your health.

Chapter One

My Personal Testimony

Indeed, we felt we received the sentence of death. But this happened that we might not rely on ourselves but on God who raises the dead.
                                                II Corinthians 1:9, NIV

I am humble as I learned the message of health the hard way. I was one of those teenage girls who struggled with my weight. It would go up and down, sometimes too far down. I would starve myself to fit into the latest fashion and then regain it all back from nutritional starvation. I would yo-yo diet as a way of life, climbing up and down the scale, which caused me to lose bone and muscle mass. As I moved through my twenties and thirties, this pattern of life continued, and my health suffered.

At the age of eighteen, I became a hair stylist and continued these unhealthy dietary patterns. By the time I was twenty-eight, I owned a beauty salon and worked as a heavy-duty colorist, breathing in many toxic chemicals and not eating properly. I had panic attacks, severe digestive issues, and drastic weight fluctuations. There was a point at which I wasn't able to hold down any food. I also had thyroid problems, chronic migraines, dizzy spells, severe bone loss, severe blood sugar issues, and kidney cancer.

The diagnosis of kidney cancer was definitely the icing on the cake for me. Medical treatment was all I knew at the time, so on March 11, 2008, I had my left kidney removed. Thank goodness, the cancer was all encapsulated, which meant that the cancer cells had not traveled anywhere else in the body. The pathology report indicated that the cancer was a direct result of my profession, because there were traces of hair dye in my kidney.

I was scared, not knowing where to turn. I prayed that God would give me my life back. I continued to suffer from many of the symptoms mentioned above. Two days after the surgery, I began praying for God to give me a sign that would lead me toward a healing path.

Although I did not have much nutritional knowledge at that time, I knew that removing an organ was not removing the cause.

In the beginning of my search for an answer, my husband and I had gone to a local health food store. There, I bumped into a bookshelf and knocked a book on the floor. As I bent down to pick up the book, I felt intense heat radiating off that book and into my hands. I knew as soon as I touched the book that it was the sign from God that would lead me to my new life. The book, *The Maker's Diet*, by Jordan S. Rubin, changed my life forever.[1] I began my healing journey.

Through Jordan's book, the Lord showed me guidelines and principles on how to heal my body that are stated clearly in scripture. I never knew that the Bible was a manual for health; I had thought it was only for spiritual needs. I started incorporating the biblically based food and lifestyle program into my life 100 percent of the time.

My body immediately began to heal from all the various health issues that plagued me. In the beginning of the biblically based program, I had gone through a detox. My body started purging what I believed was years of toxicity. My headaches, digestive problems, and blood glucose issues disappeared. In a short time, I was totally disease free and living a level of extraordinary health that I never knew existed.

The Lord then told me, "I have restored your health, and I want you to dedicate your life as the vessel to guide my children to restore their health."

I was so empowered by this command from my Lord and Savior that I wanted to share this message with others and help transform this nation and world in the same way God had healed me. I began by studying at the Biblical Health Institute, founded by Jordan Rubin, and became certified as a biblical health coach. I incorporated these life-giving services into my new wellness practice—that was once a chemical-laden hair salon—where I placed people on life giving paths to health and wellness according to God's way.

I studied as many holistic health programs as I could that relied on biblical nutrition. I then studied at the world's largest nutrition school, The Institute for Integrative Nutrition. There, I learned well over one hundred dietary theories. I also learned the connection between nature, the human body, and the mind, and how to take my practice to a level beyond what I imagined.

I have been blessed with not only total restoration in my body, but also the ability to share this information with many others and witness their transformations. I was once trapped inside a jail cell—my body. Now, I live in extraordinary health all the time.

I could not wait another minute to begin delivering to millions of people the message of health that restored me. They were suffering

---

[1] Latest version by Destiny Image Publishers, Inc., 2013.

needlessly. I began teaching holistic nutrition at a local college for adult enrichment. I have appeared on Trinity Broadcast Network (TBN) shows *Joy in Our Town* and *Doctor-to-Doctor*, discussing health and wellness.

God has used me as a transmitter of health and wellness so that I may unlock people's God-given ability to heal themselves. I educate my clients how to *stop battling disease and start building wellness.*

I asked the Lord to give me back my life. He never did; He gave me an entirely new one.

Today, I am 100 percent disease and prescription-drug free, and each day I reap the blessings of extraordinary health in the way we were all designed to live. I am the proud owner of Heaven on Earth Healing Center, Inc., where I place anyone God sends me—with any form of sickness—on the pathway to total health and healing.

I would never change my past, because it was the journey to my present and future.

> *You intended to harm me, but God intended it for good to accomplish what is now being done, the saving of many lives.*
> Genesis 50:20, NIV

I love this path that God has placed me on. I have the opportunity each day to uncover the truth about health and sickness in each person that enters my practice, enabling me to deliver the truth of health and healing that is saving so many lives. Liberating people from the ravages of sickness and the bondage of the sick care industry is so very rewarding.

It is my mission to educate God's people about the amazing benefits of real, whole, organic food. I believe that this is the medicine that prevents disease and restores health. The answer to great health is not the damaging immune-altering effects of prescription drugs and vaccines. The answer is the reconnection of nature and the human body.

I live my passion simply because it is my purpose.

Sickness is not a death sentence, but a life sentence, an opportunity to transform your own health so you can then be a testament that inspires others.

> *Rooted and built up in him, strengthened in the faith as you were taught and overflowing with thankfulness.*
> Colossians 2:7, NLV

My roots in holistic health stem back to my mom's personal interest in 1980. She planted the seeds of health in me at the age of twelve when she opened the doors of Nature's Kountry Healthy Food Store. We were one of the first health food stores during a time when there really wasn't a lot of interest in holistic health. As a result, our store closed within five years, and we, unfortunately, fled from the principles of healthy eating.

Today, I am forever grateful to God for bringing me and my family back to health and wellness. I have taken the wisdom of Grandma Fran's recipes and the seeds from my mom and replanted them in this book. I want you to understand that food doesn't have to be unhealthy in order to taste good. Healthy food prepared properly actually tastes great. Food doesn't have to make us gassy, bloated, and sick. Many of the recipes in this book have been passed down through my family's generations. All I did was switch the source of ingredients from processed, nonorganic foods to unprocessed and organic. Passing down traditions doesn't have to mean passing down sickness.

So, tie up your apron strings and make these delicious traditions—from my family to yours.

Chapter Two

What Is Organic Food?

Organic food is free of chemical fertilizers known as pesticides, fungicides, and genetic mutations. Chemical fertilizers are synthetic compounds that are not found in nature; and therefore, have the potential to affect the health of the plants as well as the humans who consume them. We should be highly concerned when we see people wearing hazmat suits spraying our food.

What about genetically modified foods?

Genetically modified foods, or GMOs, are foods that have been spliced with a gene from an unrelated species to give that food characteristics of the other species. Eating food grown through this process of gene mixing has been known to cause birth defects, organ damage, hormone disruption, and cancer. GMO foods also have a destructive effect on the ecological system, resulting in crop failure and poor-quality foods. GMOs are often grown using higher levels of toxic chemicals such as herbicides, pesticides, fertilizers, or fungicides. If you've ever used Roundup on your weeds, then you are familiar with the effects of *glyphosate,* a widely used herbicide. Now, please be aware that washing your produce doesn't wash away chemicals.

The soil is depleted of nutrients after it is drenched with these toxoids. Any food that grows relies on the soil for vitamins and minerals, and in cases like these, the foods take in all their nourishment from chemical-laden soil. So, these additives become systemic in the plant from soil and seed to full bloom and fruiting body.

Do you now have a clearer understanding of why organic ingredients are essential in these recipes?

> **Health Tip**
>
> Swap a frown for a smile and make someone's day.

Chapter Three

Eating Organic on a Budget

Organic foods are more expensive than conventional foods, making it difficult to consistently purchase them for ourselves and families. The first thing we must understand about an organic lifestyle is that it's all about abundance, not deprivation and restriction.

Organic, unprocessed, whole foods are foods the way nature intended. They are not only better tasting, but provide an abundance of nutrients that sustain us longer. Purchasing organic, whole foods may be more expensive in the checkout lane but are less expensive in the long run. You may initially save money purchasing foods that are ridden with pesticides and genetic mutations, but they can be an unfortunate way to devalue your health. These chemically produced foods actually take away from your health—due to the loss of naturally occurring vitamins and minerals caused by the disease-forming chemical cocktails that are sprayed on each crop.

Nonorganic foods are also processed with certain added chemicals that artificially stimulate your appetite, which are specifically designed to cause cravings that contribute to overeating. In the long run, you would be likely to spend *more* money as you become nutrient deficient and toxic, leading to disease. You will most likely lose money taking time off work due to sickness, as well as incur the expense of doctor visits and prescriptions.

The only thing you truly own is your body, and it's where you live. Without your health, nothing really matters. When your health is taken from you, you don't feel well enough to enjoy all the wonderful things life has to offer. I believe our health is priceless; we cannot put a price tag on it. Our health should be our biggest investment, not our last.

I want you to ask yourself: *How much am I worth?*

You are worth enough to eat healthy, organic foods. We are all worthy of eating God-made foods, so we can reap the benefits of abundant health.

Now, I do realize that a large percentage of people struggle to provide better quality food for their families. I was one of those people when I first embarked on this lifestyle. While my husband and I were transitioning into new professions, we had to start from the very bottom of an empty bank account.

With that in mind, let's take a close look at the five steps I used to provide better food for our family while on a budget. These steps will help you learn how to afford what God intended for you to eat, and you will also reap the many benefits of extraordinary health as I did. And, you won't break the bank!

1. **Shop at local farmers' markets.** Research your region for a local farmers' market or a *community supported agriculture* (CSA) organization. In a CSA, you subscribe to a *share* or agree to buy regularly allotted produce, meat, eggs, or other products from a specific farm. Before you sign up, I suggest you do your research: get to know your farmers and ask what may be sprayed on the food that you're buying since *local* doesn't necessarily mean *organic*. Meat and dairy should always be purchased from a local farm that doesn't engage in inhumane practices or pump their animals full of antibiotics and growth hormones. Remember, we are not only what we eat, but what our food eats.

   Since foods from the CSA or the booths at a farmers' market grow right in your area, the farmer saves traveling fees, which lowers the cost. This is a great way to get high quality food at a reasonable price. It's a win-win for you and the farmer.

2. **Remove costly junk foods from your menu.** By removing these foods as well as all the many other products that are robbing your health, you free money to purchase foods that restore your health.

3. **Cook at home.** When you cook in your own kitchen, you save money since you don't have to tip a waiter or pay high prices for low quality foods. You also have control of the source of your ingredients.

4. **Search for coupons and discounts.** Almost everyone is on the internet nowadays, so take advantage and print out organic product coupons. Companies are always giving coupons to promote their products. Take flyers from your local health food store, cut out the coupons, and save a bundle. Every little bit counts. Go to allnaturalsavings.com or naturalthrifty.com for coupons on organic products. Additionally, most health food stores offer bonuses and discounts after spending a certain amount of money, so I encourage you to inquire about this money-saving strategy. You may be able to order case lots at deep discounts. If a case it too much for

your family to buy at once, consider going in on an order with friends or neighbors.

5. **Grow your own food.** Having a garden can be fun and rewarding. You can also explore community gardens where you can share the work and trade your food with others.

Where there is a will, there's a way. I always believe that God blesses our steps by opening doors that we never believed would open for us. Taking care of our temples, our bodies, is one of God's commands.

Eating in this healthy way also contributes to the better health of our planet, blessing future generations. It is our spiritual responsibility to take care of the land as well as our bodies.

> *I know your deeds. See, I have placed before you an open door that no one can shut. I know that you have little strength, yet you have kept my word and have not denied my name.*
> Revelation 3:8, NIV

> *You shall not pollute the land in which you live, for blood pollutes the land, and no atonement can be made for the land for the blood that is shed in it, except by the blood of the one who shed it.*
> Numbers 35:33, ESV

My Personal Testimony

Before I knew how sick I really was, I had a successful hair salon and my husband had an awesome job as top manager of a company. We vacationed twice a year, and my daughter had everything she needed and wanted. I had never thought for one moment that my life would change to the point where I would be sick and not know where my next dime was coming from.

I was stripped of everything, I could no longer style hair because the chemicals were making me sick, and my husband lost his job in the same week that I received the diagnosis of cancer. We went through all our savings and were left financially broke. Our spirits were broken. When I cried out to God for an answer, He spoke to my heart and lead me to scripture. I then began to learn the true meaning of healthy eating.

Although I was so amazed and excited with the long-awaited information I was finding, I was afraid that I wouldn't be able to afford the foods and supplements that I needed for my healing. The fear that came over me was overwhelming because I knew in my heart of hearts that this was the answer to reverse the conditions I was suffering. I also knew that God was using me for something great, and I needed to get healthy, so I could be an instrument of health to inspire others to do the same.

> *The pain that you've been feeling, can't compare to the joy that's coming.*
> Romans 8:18 (paraphrased)

I knew as a little girl that I was going to do something exceptionally great one day through leadership. I knew that I would speak in front of many people and not only lead by example, but bring truth that would set many free. God gave me a passion to help others, which led me to my purpose.

I reflected back on that childhood knowledge, let go of the fear, and stepped into faith. How could I ever allow fear to take over my childhood dream that was ordained by God? The best thing that God could have ever done for me was to strip me of everything so that I could become a clean slate and allow God to rebuild me from the bottom up.

> *Trust in the LORD with all your heart and lean not on your own understanding. In all thy ways acknowledge him, and he shall direct your paths.*
> Proverbs 3:5–6, NIV

As I began to learn more about health and healing, I trusted in God with all my heart and was able to afford the necessities to move forward.

I now can be all that God has called me to be.

Today, not only do I experience extraordinary health each day, I have a successful practice, have appeared on numerous health shows, own my home free and clear, and am a best-selling author. More importantly, I am able to bless forward to those in need. I thank God for placing me on this path that restored my health and finances and allows me to be a vessel and transmitter of health and wellness to others.

> *Now faith is the substance of things hoped for, the evidence of things not seen.*
> Hebrews 11:1, KJV

Although there may be plenty of strategies on how to eat organic on a budget, first and foremost we must always trust God who lives and dwells in us by stepping into faith and believing. Allow God to strip you of everything, so He can rebuild you as He did with me. God gave us dominion over the earth. When we believe in Jesus, we do greater works than He did.

> *I tell you the truth, anyone who believes in me will do the same works I have done, and even greater works . . .*
> John 14:12, NLT

> *Then God said, "Let us make humankind in our image, according to our likeness; and let them have dominion over the fish of the sea, and over the birds of the air, and over the cattle, and over all the wild animals of the earth, and over every creeping*

thing that creeps upon the earth." So, God created humankind in his image, in the image of God.

Genesis 1:26-28, NKJV

Fear Not

Do not be afraid, for I have ransomed you. I have called you by name; you are mine.

Isaiah 43:1, NLT

So much of my life I lived in constant fear. This fearful thought was brought on from never feeling well, due to my poor eating habits.

I was always worrying that something must be seriously wrong. At times, I even feared that I was going to die. I had such a will to live, so much to live for, and dreams that had not yet been fulfilled.

In addition to changing my poor eating habits, I attribute a large part of my healing to the understanding that there are also spiritual roots that lead to disease. I discovered that the spiritual root of kidney issues is fear, and I so desperately needed to cast my fears to my Heavenly Father.

God spoke to my heart and said, "I did not give you a spirit of fear. I gave you power and love and a sound mind." He told me that he has many great plans for my life and that my life was far from over.

For God has not given us a spirit of fear, but of power and of love and a sound mind.

2 Timothy 1:7, NHEB

I cried out to the Lord and asked him to remove this constant worry and fear and he delivered me, almost instantly. I went from fear to faith and realized, like the saying, that *F.E.A.R* was just *false evidence, appearing real*. I went from a worrier to a warrior, and I knew there was a reason for all the emotional and physical pain that I had endured.

The righteous cry out and the LORD hears them; he delivers them from all their troubles. The LORD is close to the brokenhearted and saves those who are crushed in spirit.

Psalms 34:17, 18 NIV

I hope I have inspired you to take a leap of faith and trust in God for your finances as well as your health because God did not give us a spirit of fear. When we minister to others with our healthy temples, we need real food to live well. God blesses our steps because we trust and have faith in him, He always restores; I am living proof of this.

Chapter Four

Breaking Your Fast

Most people head straight to the kitchen after a good night's sleep to *break* their *fast* with breakfast. Your sleeping hours are considered a fast because you've refrained from eating during that time. Is this meal to break your fast really something you should consume as soon as you see the light of day?

Breaking your fast should be done with approximately 16–20 ounces of filtered water (with 1 tablespoon of apple cider vinegar and the juice of one half lemon) to hydrate your cells and prepare the body for food. Water allows the organs to wake up and be ready for proper digestion. Drinking water before you eat also fuels your metabolism and helps you stay regular. Morning water consumption flushes your body of the toxins that lead to cravings and overeating, so you won't be as hungry when you do eat.

What are you breaking your fast with? After hydrating your cells with filtered water, wait at least an hour before you munch down that meal. This will give your digestion time to create the necessary enzymes for proper assimilation of food. Enzymes are catalysts that help us break down fats, carbohydrates, and proteins.

Okay, calm down—I promise you will not starve, and you'll actually feel better. You will even have more energy in addition to all the other great aspects of drinking water. At this point I'm sure you're wondering what exactly you should eat for that morning meal since your usual breakfast menu consisted of a bagel with cream cheese, or perhaps a doughnut.

After reading my first book, you've learned about intermittent fasting but let's just go over exactly what this type of fast means. *Intermittent fasting* means you refrain from taking in food for 12–18 hours during the day to give the body a rest. This resting time allows the body to heal from the toxic overload of over-eating, chemical fertilizers, gas, bloating, unwanted weight gain, and even certain types of sickness.

We Must Stop Battling Disease and Start Building Wellness.

Before we dive into the recipes in each chapter, I want you to understand that, because eating is actually how you fuel your body, food sources *do* matter. Nonorganic food sources have the potential to keep your body in a constant battle. Organically sourced ingredients allow the food to deliver optimal taste and nutrition, making them your greatest weapon against disease.

For each recipe, please use 100 percent organic ingredients for optimal flavor and highest nutritional value.

Breakfast

Tonijean's Hearty Oatmeal	35
Tri-Color Quinoa Breakfast Porridge	37
Cinnamon Banana Walnut Pancakes	39
Gluten-Free Blueberry Muffins	41
Easy Egg Frittata	42
Einkorn Blueberry Pancakes	43
Fluffy Coconut Pancakes	44
Grandma Fran's Odd Egg Dish	45

Chapter

Five

"All photographs in this book courtesy of Vladimir Kulpinski, photographygonegreen.com"

Tonijean's Hearty Oatmeal

Makes 2 servings

*Good morning and welcome to the breakfast table.
Let's start with a delicious and hearty bowl of oatmeal.*

Directions

Mix together the oats, water, and kefir or yogurt. Cover with cheesecloth or paper towel and let stand at room temperature overnight in a stainless steel or cast iron pot. (The kefir may affect the seasoning of the cast iron.)

In the morning, add the milk. Stir well on medium heat for about 3 minutes, just enough to warm up your oats. Stir frequently to prevent sticking. Add the ghee or butter or coconut oil, salt, walnuts, maple syrup, cinnamon, vanilla extract, dates, and blueberries. Mix well and enjoy!

Ingredients

1 cup rolled oats
2 cups filtered water
1 Tbsp plain kefir, whole-milk kefir or whole plain yogurt
½ cup whole milk of choice
1 Tbsp grass-fed butter or ghee (clarified butter)
Or 1 Tbsp coconut butter (manna) or coconut oil
4 pitted dates, halved
½ cup blueberries
Pinch unrefined salt
1 Tbsp real maple syrup (or more)
⅛ tsp Ceylon cinnamon
1 tsp vanilla extract
¼ cup raw walnuts

Health Tip

You may add any fresh fruit to this recipe. I like to add a chopped banana or fresh berries. Any raw nuts can also be used. I prefer walnuts in my oatmeal for their sweet, smooth, and buttery flavor.

Tri-Color Quinoa Breakfast Porridge

Makes 2 servings

Directions

Follow directions on package and prepare quinoa.

Add all other ingredients to cooked quinoa. Mix well and serve.

* Please see the Resource section for recommended brands and their availability.

Ingredients

½ cup Truroots* uncooked, sprouted quinoa trio
½ cup raw unsalted pistachios, shelled
1 Tbsp extra virgin coconut oil or coconut butter (a.k.a. manna)
⅛ tsp unrefined salt
⅛ tsp Ceylon cinnamon
1 pinch powdered nutmeg
1 tsp vanilla extract
¼ cup unsweetened dried cranberries
¼ cup pure maple syrup or raw honey

Cinnamon Banana Walnut Pancakes

Makes 6–8 pancakes

Directions

Option 1: Place all ingredients in blender and mix well for 1–2 minutes.

Option 2: Hand mix the wet ingredients in a medium bowl, then add the dry ingredients and mix well.

Melt coconut oil or coconut butter in a preheated griddle or stainless pan over medium-low heat. Ladle about 3 tablespoons of batter onto surface for each pancake. The pancakes should be 2–3 inches in diameter and thick. Cook for a few minutes on each side. Flip over when one side starts to turn slightly brown. Cook for a total of approximately 5 minutes. Top with melted coconut butter, real maple syrup, and cinnamon.

Ingredients

- 1 cup extra-fine almond flour
- ½ cup tapioca flour
- 1 tsp baking soda
- ⅛ tsp unrefined salt
- 2 medium bananas, ripe
- 1 Tbsp coconut butter, melted
- 1 Tbsp real maple syrup
- ½ cup almond or coconut milk (add bit more for thinner pancakes, less for thicker pancakes)
- 1 Tbsp vanilla extract
- 1 tsp Ceylon cinnamon
- ½ cup raw walnuts
- Coconut oil or red palm oil (for sautéing)

Gluten-Free Blueberry Muffins

Makes 6 large or 12 medium muffins

Directions

Preheat oven to 350°F. Grease large 6–8 muffin pan with coconut oil or butter. Option: use large muffin cups.

Mix dry ingredients in a bowl. In a separate bowl, whisk together eggs, maple syrup or raw honey, and vanilla. Add to dry ingredients and blend thoroughly. Gently fold in blueberries, then pour batter into 6–8 large cups. Bake for 30 minutes. After the muffins come out of the oven, cool on rack for 10 minutes. Enjoy with softened butter, ghee, or plain.

Ingredients

- 2 cups almond flour
- ½ cup coconut flour
- 6 pasture-raised eggs
- ½ cup real maple syrup or raw honey
- ¾ tsp vanilla extract or raw honey
- ½ tsp unrefined salt
- 1 cup frozen or fresh blueberries
- 1 Tbsp butter or ghee
- Extra virgin coconut oil (for greasing muffin pan)

Easy Egg Frittata

Makes 4 servings

Directions

Preheat oven to 350ºF. Grease bottom only of 9-inch round baking pan with coconut oil. Mix all ingredients in a bowl. Pour mixture into the greased pan. Bake for 25 minutes. Slice and serve. This dish also makes a great lunch or dinner served with a side salad.

Ingredients

1 Tbsp coconut oil
10 eggs
Seven to eight ½-inch pieces of raw cheddar or any raw cheese of choice
1 cup fresh, cooked, or frozen broccoli
2 Tbsp Locatelli* Pecorino Romano sheep cheese, grated
Pinch of black pepper
Pinch of unrefined salt
⅛ tsp powdered garlic
⅛ tsp powdered onion

Health Tip

Wherever refined salt is called for in recipes, substitute real, unrefined Celtic or Himalayan salt and get life-giving minerals back into your body.

Einkorn Blueberry Pancakes

Makes 4 pancakes

*Start your morning with my blueberry pancakes.
These will be a hit in your home. Please share the love!*

Directions

Mix dry ingredients together first. Then, stir in wet ingredients to make a thick batter. In a medium stainless pan, add 1 teaspoon coconut oil or 1 tablespoon butter, and add approximately 3 tablespoons of batter. Cook 2 minutes on each side.

Serve with butter, maple syrup, or coconut syrup and fresh fruit of choice.

* Please see the Resource section for recommended brands and their availability.

Ingredients

1 cup all-purpose einkorn flour*
2 large pasture-raised eggs
½ cup full-fat, real coconut milk
Or ½ cup full-fat dairy milk
1 ripe banana, mashed
1 tsp vanilla extract
1½ Tbsp of Bob's Red Mill* coconut flour
½ tsp Ceylon cinnamon
½ cup fresh or frozen blueberries
¼ tsp nonaluminum baking soda
1 small pinch of unrefined salt
Ghee or coconut oil (for frying)

Fluffy Coconut Pancakes

Makes 6 pancakes

Wake up to fluffy coconut pancakes!

Directions

In a medium bowl, mash the banana well. Beat eggs until frothy, about 2 minutes, then add to the bananas. Mix in the milk, vanilla, maple syrup, and raw honey.

In a separate medium-sized bowl, combine the coconut flour, baking soda, and unrefined salt and whisk together.

Stir the wet mixture into the dry mixture until the dry ingredients are well incorporated.

Preheat griddle or stainless steel pan over medium-low heat. Add coconut oil or butter for frying. Ladle about 3 tablespoons of batter into pan for each pancake. The pancakes should be 2–3 inches in diameter and thick. Cook for a few minutes until the edges turn slightly brown, then flip . Cook for about 5 minutes in total. Top with raw or organic butter, real maple syrup, fresh fruit, and cinnamon.

Yummy!

Ingredients

4 pasture-raised eggs, at room temperature
1 cup milk (raw cow milk or coconut milk works well)
2 tsp vanilla extract
1 Tbsp raw honey
1 ripe banana
1 Tbsp real maple syrup
½ cup coconut flour
1 tsp baking soda
⅛ tsp unrefined salt
1 Tbsp extra virgin coconut oil or butter for frying

Grandma Fran's Odd Egg Dish

My brother, Richard, granted me permission to include this recipe and wrote about his memories of it. He writes:

From the first moment Grandma Fran's delicious, yet simple, sunny-side up egg dish touched my lips, it has stayed fondly in my heart. I am unsure if anyone has ever had a similar dish, but this was considered a peasant food many years ago. As a young boy, this dish always stood out to me, mixing eggs with peas and leftover tomato sauce seemed a bit odd. However, after trying it, I couldn't get enough. Coming from an Italian family, we always had leftover tomato sauce, and peas were an important protein staple in our home. Grandma Frances took those ingredients, added eggs, and made a meal.

Directions

Heat a small, stainless skillet on medium setting, then add olive oil and allow oil to heat. Crack 2 eggs into pan and cook for 90 seconds. Add peas and tomato sauce, cover with lid, and adjust to low heat. Let cook for 3 minutes. Adjust the time slightly to leave yolks loose or more solid. Add salt and pepper to taste. Sprinkle grated cheese on top and serve hot.

Ingredients

2 eggs
1 cup leftover tomato sauce (*Pomodoro* sauce from page 129)
½ cup peas, cooked
1 Tbsp extra virgin olive oil
Unrefined salt and black pepper to taste
1 Tbsp raw, hard cheese, grated

Soups

Hearty Tri-Color Lentil Soup	49
Creamy Butternut Squash Soup	51
Delicious, Creamy Sweet Potato Soup	53
Hearty Chicken Vegetable Soup	55
Siberian Lamb Soup	56
Hearty Vegetable Soup with Quinoa	57
Healing Mineral Soup	58

Chapter

Six

Hearty Tri-Color Lentil Soup

Makes 6–8 servings

When it's super cold outside, most of us desire a hearty, hot bowl of soup. It can't get any heartier than my lentil soup with kale. This soup is full of vitamins and minerals and high in protein but most importantly, it's delicious.

Directions

Add all other ingredients to a large stainless pot. Simmer on low for 2½ hours, stirring occasionally. Serve as is or with freshly made quinoa, prepared by following directions on the package.

Always add a full cup of love!

* Please see the Resource section for recommended brands and their availability.

Ingredients

4 quarts filtered water or broth
8-ounce package TruRoots* quinoa, cooked separately
1 bag of TruRoots* tri-color sprouted lentils
2 Tbsp raw coconut oil
2 stalks celery, chopped
2 large carrots, chopped
1 small onion, diced small
4 or 5 garlic cloves, minced
1 apple, chopped small
3 large bay leaves
2 Tbsp fresh thyme, chopped
¼ cup fresh parsley, chopped
Unrefined salt to taste
Black pepper to taste

Creamy Butternut Squash Soup

Makes 4 servings as entrée, 8 servings as side

*As the leaves start to change and the air becomes brisk,
warm up your home with my creamy,
butternut squash soup.*

Directions

Place all ingredients in large stainless steel pot and cook on medium heat for 35 minutes, stirring frequently. Cook until vegetables are tender and then blend until creamy. Serve hot with an additional sage leaf.

Serve as a side to any meal or as a full meal with your choice of salad from Chapter Seven.

Ingredients

4 cups fresh or frozen butternut squash, cubed
Or 2 (15 or 16 ounce) cans of plain, sweet, butternut purée
2 apples, peeled, cored, diced
1 small onion, chopped
2 large carrots, chopped
1 (13.5 ounces) can Native Forest* coconut milk (full fat)
½ cup apple cider
½ cup real maple syrup
2 garlic cloves, minced
2 Tbsp raw honey
½ tsp powdered onion
½ tsp powdered garlic
1 Tbsp Ceylon cinnamon
½ tsp powered ginger
1½ tsp powdered nutmeg
3 leaves fresh sage
Unrefined salt to taste
Black pepper to taste

Options:

With a desire for butternut squash soup as winter approached, I played around with this recipe and two other recipes were created. For two other delicious soups, change out the butternut squash and replace it with delicious pumpkin or sweet potato. The other ingredients are the same.

- For *pumpkin soup*, I used 2 (15 or 16 ounce) cans plain pumpkin or 4 cups cooked, fresh pumpkin in place of the butternut squash and followed the recipe.

- For *sweet potato soup*, I used 2 (15 or 16 ounce) cans plain sweet potato purée, or 4 cups cooked, fresh sweet potato in place of the butternut squash and followed the recipe.

Soups on!

* Please see the Resource section for recommended brands and their availability.

Delicious, Creamy Sweet Potato Soup

Makes 4–6 servings

Directions

Add the sweet potatoes, apples, garlic, and onion into a blender or food processor and purée. Place the mixture into a pot on medium heat. Add unrefined salt and black pepper to taste, then add in the carrots, coconut cream or milk, cinnamon, nutmeg, and ginger. As soup is cooking, add in the coconut oil. Pour in the vegetable or chicken broth and simmer for about 15 minutes.

Serve with love!

Ingredients

2 (15 or 16 ounce) cans sweet potato purée
Or fresh sweet potatoes (medium size), diced with skins on
2 apples, seeds removed, skin on, diced
2 garlic cloves
1 small onion, chopped
2 carrots, chopped
1 13. 5 ounce can full-fat coconut cream or milk
1 tsp Ceylon cinnamon
1 tsp nutmeg
½ tsp grated ginger
1 heaping Tbsp extra virgin coconut oil
2 cups vegetable or chicken broth
Unrefined salt
Black pepper

Hearty Chicken Vegetable Soup

Makes 4–6 servings

Directions

Add all ingredients to a large pot, including whole chicken. Cook for 3 hours. Carefully remove chicken and debone, checking remaining soup for stray bones and skin. Add chicken and parsley to soup. Stir and place lid on pot for several minutes. Serve.

*The raw apple cider vinegar extracts the marrow into the broth for healthy digestion.

Ingredients

1 whole pasture-raised, organic chicken
3 cups kale, chopped
1 onion, chopped
5 garlic cloves, diced
3 celery stalks, chopped coarsely
2 cups butternut squash, peeled and diced
2 medium-sized sweet potatoes, chopped with skin on
1 bunch parsley, chopped
3 large carrots, chopped with skin on
4 tomatoes, puréed
1 Tbsp garlic powder
1 Tbsp onion powder
3 quarts spring water
3 Tbsp raw apple cider vinegar*
Black pepper to taste
Unrefined salt to taste

Siberian Lamb Soup

Makes 6 servings

Although my husband, Vladimir, is from the Ukraine, he always enjoys a steaming, hot bowl of Siberian Lamb soup. The frigid winter months of the Ukraine call for hot soup, and Siberian Lamb soup hits the spot. Here's my husband's version of Siberian Lamb soup.

Directions

Fill a large stainless pot almost to the top with water. Add all the ingredients except for the sour cream and boil for 3 hours. Serve topped with sour cream.

Enjoy!

Ingredients

5 pounds pasture-raised lamb shanks
5 large carrots, diced
2 stalks celery, chopped
1 medium onion, diced
5 garlic cloves, minced
1 small bunch parsley, chopped
1 small bunch fresh dill, chopped
1 large (18.3 ounce) jar diced tomatoes
1 Tbsp garlic powder
1 Tbsp onion powder
4 small red or yellow potatoes, diced
1 Tbsp unrefined salt
1 tsp black pepper
½ tsp cayenne pepper
Dollop of sour cream

Hearty Vegetable Soup with Quinoa

Makes 6–8 servings

Directions

Add water to large pot and bring to a simmer. Add the quinoa and let cook while preparing the rest of the vegetables. Add the tomatoes, onion, garlic, celery, sweet potatoes, carrots, and broccoli. Continue to boil for 40 minutes.

When veggies and quinoa are tender, stir in basil, rosemary, and celery seeds. Remove from heat. While cooling, add lemon juice. Add fresh scallions and optional coconut meat. Season to taste with unrefined salt and pepper.

Ingredients

8 cups filtered water
½ cup uncooked quinoa
1 (18.3 ounce) can diced tomatoes
1 large onion, chopped
3 stalks celery, chopped
2 cloves garlic, chopped
4 large carrots (or 6 medium), unpeeled and sliced
3 large sweet potatoes, unpeeled and cut into chunks
1 cup broccoli, chopped
1 tsp basil
1 tsp rosemary
1 tsp celery seeds
1 tsp lemon juice
Unrefined salt
Freshly ground black pepper
¼ cup fresh scallions, chopped (optional)
¼ cup coconut meat, diced (optional)

Healing Mineral Soup

Makes 8–10 servings

When you're feeling a bit under the weather, or even a lot under the weather, you may very well need a mineral boost. Minerals help restore digestion, increase healthy bone and muscle mass, reduce inflammation, relieve pain, soothe a sore throat, and comfort a tummy ache.

Directions

In a large stainless pot, add all the ingredients and cook on medium heat for 40 minutes and serve hot. Store in refrigerator for up to 5 days or freeze up to 6 months.

* Please see the Resource section for recommended brands and their availability.

Ingredients

2 quarts water
2 cups shiitake mushrooms, chopped with stems
½ green cabbage, finely chopped
½ cup fennel, chopped
1 Tbsp fresh ginger, grated
3 large carrots, thinly sliced
3 celery stalks, thinly sliced
4 garlic cloves, thinly sliced
2 scallions, chopped small
4 large bay leaves
½ cup fresh cilantro or parsley, chopped
2 Tbsp South River Miso Company*garlic red pepper miso
1 tsp powdered garlic
1 tsp powdered onion
1 tsp coarse black pepper
1 tsp unrefined salt

Health Tip

Swap hydrogenated, disease-forming canola, corn, and soy oils for extra virgin coconut or red palm oil for cooking and smoothies.

Salads

Potato Salad: Three Ways	61
Quinoa Salad with Chickpeas	63
High-Energy Healing Salad	65
Mango and Watermelon Salad	67
Beet Salad	69
Popeye's Spinach Salad	71
The Sweetest Potato Salad	73
Red Cabbage Salad	75
Grandma Fran's Wild Flounder Salad	77
Grandma Fran's String Bean Salad	78
Matthew Clark's Sweet, Crunchy, Delicious Salad	79
Arame Salad	81
Warm Arame Salad	82
Kale and Sweet Potato Salad	82
What's in the Fridge Salad	83
Arugula and Pear Salad with Feta	85
Mediterranean Arugula Salad with Heirloom Tomatoes	86
High-Protein Kale Salad	87
High-Protein Pasta Salad	88
High-Enzymatic Salad	89
Creamy Ranch Dressing	91
High-Antioxidant Salad Dressing	92

Chapter

Seven

Potato Salad: Three Ways

Makes 6 Servings

Potatoes are one of the most nutrient-rich foods on the planet. They are packed with fiber, loaded with antioxidants, and contain some of the most important minerals such as, magnesium, selenium, iron, and zinc. One medium-sized potato provides 50–60 milligrams of vitamin C and has more potassium than a banana. Potatoes are high in all B vitamins, which include: B_1, B_3, B_6, and B_{12}.

Variation One:

Directions

Cover potatoes with water in pot. On medium heat, boil potatoes with lid on about 25 minutes, until tender. Remove from heat, drain water, and then chill in the refrigerator for 20 minutes. After potatoes are cold, add onions, garlic, olive oil, vinegar, salt and pepper, and fresh parsley. Mix well and serve. Keep in airtight container for up to 3 days.

Variation Two:

Follow the recipe above, substituting ¼ cup fresh chopped cilantro for ¼ cup chopped parsley. Add the juice of one lime. Everything else remains the same.

Variation Three:

Follow the recipe above, substituting ¼ cup fresh chopped dill for ¼ cup parsley. Add one Tablespoon whole-milk sour cream. Everything else remains the same.

Ingredients

6 medium red potatoes, quartered, skin on
1 medium yellow onion, thinly sliced
1 clove garlic, minced
3 Tbsp extra virgin olive oil
1 Tbsp raw apple cider vinegar
½ tsp black pepper
½ tsp unrefined salt
¼ cup fresh parsley, chopped

Quinoa Salad with Chickpeas

Makes 4 Servings

Who says plants don't have protein? Plants have just as much protein as meat, if not more. Protein is a chain of amino acids essential in every living thing; and therefore, meat is recycled plant protein. Quinoa is a complete protein.

Directions

Prepare quinoa according to package directions. Remove from heat and set aside to cool.

Combine all other ingredients in a bowl. Pour on top of quinoa and mix. Serve immediately or cover and chill in the fridge.

Enjoy!

Ingredients

1 cup dry quinoa
2 Tbsp fresh parsley, chopped
2 Tbsp fresh chives, chopped
½ cup red seedless grapes, halved
⅓ cup pecans, chopped (or nut of choice)
⅓ cup dried cranberries
1 cup chickpeas, soaked and cooked
2 Tbsp lemon juice, freshly squeezed (about 1 large lemon)
2 Tbsp olive oil
1 Tbsp raw apple cider vinegar

Freshly ground black pepper to taste
Unrefined salt to taste

Health Tip

Swap anger and unforgiveness for love, peace, forgiveness, and joy.

High-Energy Healing Salad

Makes 4 Servings

Try this anti-inflammatory, anticancer, healing salad.

Directions

Toss all ingredients and enjoy!

* Please see the Resource section for recommended brands and their availability.

Ingredients

3 cups mixed greens
½ cup pea sprouts
8 cherry tomatoes, halved
½ cup chickpeas
1 red onion, chopped
1 avocado, diced
½ cup bean sprouts
1 Tbsp kelp flakes
⅛ tsp garlic powder
2 Tbsp Coconut Secret* coconut aminos
2 tsp Coconut Secret* coconut vinegar
3 Tbsp hemp seed oil

Unrefined salt to taste

Mango and Watermelon Salad

Makes 4–6 servings as a side

Cool off on a hot day with my refreshing mango and watermelon salad.

Directions

In a large bowl, add all ingredients. Add feta cheese, if desired. Mix well and serve.

Ingredients

2 cups fresh watermelon, cut into bite-sized chunks (remove seeds)
1 cup fresh mango, cut into bite-sized chunks
1 small red onion, sliced thin
¼ cup fresh cilantro, chopped
¼ cup fresh mint, chopped
¼ cup shredded, unsweetened coconut
1 large cucumber with skin, sliced thin
1 Tbsp hemp seed oil
3 Tbsp extra virgin olive oil
1 Tbsp coconut vinegar
Juice of 1 orange, freshly squeezed
⅛ tsp powdered garlic
Black pepper to taste
Unrefined salt to taste
½ cup fresh feta cheese, crumbled (optional)

Beet Salad

Makes 8 Servings

My husband enjoyed this delicious beet salad many times as a child growing up in the Ukraine. When he first made it for our family, it quickly became a favorite at the Kulpinski residence.

Directions

Boil whole potatoes separately, leaving a slight crunch to them. Set aside to cool. After they cool, cut them into bite sized pieces, removing the skin if you prefer. (I prefer the skin on since the skin contains a ton of nutrients.)

In another pot, boil the red beets whole so they retain their juice. Cook the beets until tender. Let cool, then cut into bite-sized pieces similar to the size of the cut potatoes. Add both to a bowl large enough for all the ingredients.

Dice the entire yellow onion, cut the pickles into ¼-inch pieces, and finely chop the dill. Add all remaining ingredients to beet and potato bowl, mix well, and serve as a side dish to complement any meal.

Ingredients

3–4 medium red potatoes
5–6 small to medium red beets
1 medium yellow onion
2 large dill pickles
1 cup cooked black beans (or any type of bean)
2 Tbsp fresh dill, chopped (optional)
1 Tbsp raw apple cider vinegar
3–4 Tbsp extra virgin olive oil

Unrefined salt to taste
Black pepper to taste

Popeye's Spinach Salad

Makes 2 Servings

Directions

Mix all ingredients in a large bowl.

Toss with love and serve.

Ingredients

2 cups fresh spinach
8 cherry tomatoes, halved
1 small red onion, chopped
7–10 Mediterranean olives
6 raw asparagus spears, chopped
12 sun-dried tomatoes, halved
1 cup fresh papaya, chopped
½ cucumber, sliced thin
1 Tbsp capers
½ cup garbanzo beans, cooked and cooled
5–6 artichoke hearts (from a jar)
1 ripe avocado, diced
3 Tbsp extra virgin olive oil
1 Tbsp raw apple cider vinegar
⅛ tsp powdered garlic
⅛ tsp powdered onion

Unrefined salt to taste
Black pepper to taste

The Sweetest Potato Salad

Makes 8 servings

Directions

Leaving the skins on, boil the sweet potatoes and set aside to cool. Cut potatoes into bite-sized pieces.

In another bowl, add the rest of the ingredients and mix well. Add this mixture to the sweet potatoes and toss well. Chill for 1 hour before serving.

Ingredients

6 large sweet potatoes
1 cup raw walnuts, chopped
1 small red onion, chopped
1 tsp fresh grated ginger
1 tsp Ceylon cinnamon
1 tsp dried nutmeg
2 Tbsp unrefined flaxseed oil
½ cup extra virgin olive oil
3 Tbsp raw apple cider vinegar
¼ cup fresh cilantro or parsley, chopped
½ cup real maple syrup

Unrefined salt to taste
Black pepper to taste

Red Cabbage Salad

Makes 6 Servings

Directions

Place ingredients in bowl.

Whisk dressing ingredients—all to your taste.

Add dressing to vegetable mix. Squeeze the juice of a fresh lemon on top, mix with love, and serve.

Ingredients

1 medium red cabbage, sliced into bite-sized pieces
1 small yellow or red onion, diced
1 medium apple, diced fine with skin
10 cherry tomatoes, halved
1 yellow or orange pepper, diced small
1 stalk celery, diced
½ cucumber, diced
½ zucchini, diced
1 whole carrot, shredded
1 lemon

Dressing

½ cup extra virgin olive oil
1 Tbsp coconut vinegar
Black pepper to taste
Unrefined salt to taste
Garlic powder to taste

Grandma Fran's Wild Flounder Salad

Makes 4 Servings

While Grandma Frances would be leaning over her bedroom window hanging her clothes on the clothesline, the scent of fresh garlic from her fish salad would fill the air of her kitchen.

Directions

Boil fish for 5–7 minutes in a large stainless pot with enough water to cover fish. After fish is cooked, drain water and chill fish in refrigerator for 30 minutes or longer. In a large bowl, add cooked and chilled fish, onions, garlic, parsley, oil, vinegar, parsley, salt, and pepper. Mix lightly without breaking fish and serve as a side or a meal.

My grandma would serve this with bread and her string bean salad, which can be found below in the next recipe.

Ingredients

1½ pounds fresh wild flounder or cod
½ cup fresh parsley, chopped
3–4 Tbsp extra virgin olive oil
1 Tbsp raw apple cider vinegar
1 small yellow onion, sliced thin
2–3 cloves fresh garlic, sliced thin

Unrefined salt to taste
Freshly crushed black pepper to taste

Grandma Fran's String Bean Salad

Makes 6–8 Servings

I always looked forward to my grandma's cold string bean salad because I got to help her break the string beans in half, and I loved to eat them raw. Her salad was savory, yet sweet, and packed a nice crunch on a hot summer day.

Directions

Cook potatoes until tender, then cut into bite-sized pieces, leave skin on if you prefer. Chill in refrigerator for 30 minutes.

Boil green beans for approximately 5 minutes, leaving them crunchy (al denté). Do not overcook. Chill in refrigerator for 30 minutes.

In large bowl, add potatoes and string beans, onions, parsley, basil, oregano, olive oil, vinegar, salt, and pepper. Mix well.

Refrigerate 30 minutes. Serve with *Grandma Fran's Wild Flounder Salad* as the main dish or as a side to another meal.

Ingredients

5–6 medium red potatoes
2 pounds fresh string beans, ends removed, snapped in half
1 large yellow onion, sliced thin
¼ cup fresh basil, chopped
½ cup parsley, chopped
1 sprig dried or fresh oregano
½ cup extra virgin olive oil
2 Tbsp raw apple cider vinegar
Unrefined salt to taste
Black pepper to taste

Matthew Clark's Sweet, Crunchy, Delicious Salad

Makes 4 Servings

With permission from my friend, Matthew Clark. He says:

I love this salad because it is so simple and easy to make. It tastes incredible. It always leaves a fresh taste in your mouth and a satisfied feeling after eating—especially, if you like sweet stuff.

It's the perfect combination of sweet, crunchy, salty, and deliciousness. The dressing is the last piece to finish off the puzzle, leaving you feeling like all your senses have been taken care of.

It is a great salad to have by itself or to accompany a beautiful piece of fish, chicken, or steak. Whatever your flavor, this will be a winning recipe for you or to impress your friends and family.

Directions

Whisk dressing ingredients together in a medium bowl. Set aside.

In a large salad bowl, add mixed the greens, mandarin slices, strawberries, peppers, pumpkin seeds, cucumber, tomatoes, and avocado. Add the salad dressing and grated cheese. Toss and serve.

Ingredients

4 cups mixed greens
1 cup Mandarin orange slices, fresh or canned
½ cup strawberries, thinly sliced
½ cup red and yellow pepper, diced
¼ cup pumpkin seeds
1 cucumber, thinly sliced
2 Roma tomatoes, diced
1 avocado, cubed
½ cup Parmesan cheese, coarsely grated

Dressing

¼ cup fresh mint, chopped
¼ cup fresh basil, chopped
1 tsp fresh rosemary, chopped
¼ cup fresh parsley, chopped
½ cup extra virgin olive oil
2 Tbsp balsamic vinegar
1 Tbsp raw honey

Unrefined salt to taste
Black pepper to taste

Arame Salad

Makes 4 servings

With permission from Garden Café
A delicious, organic restaurant in Woodstock, New York
Lea Fridrich, Proprietress

Directions

Empty the package of arame into a large bowl and cover with warm water. Pull it apart, making sure it is all submerged. Set it aside to soak for about half an hour. Note: a little more or less than 30 minutes is okay.

While arame is soaking, prepare your vegetables. Cut the top and bottom ends off the red onion, cut down the middle, and then place flat side down to thinly slice.

Peel the carrot and use the larger holes of a box grater to shred.

Cut a green cabbage in half and remove the stem. Place the flat side down and slice thinly. You could also use the slicing side of the box grater.

Mix all three vegetables together in another bowl with the brown rice vinegar and sesame oil. Massage the vegetables with your hands and then set aside to wilt a little.

Carefully strain the arame in a colander and rinse under cool water. Add the arame to the vegetables. Add the tamari and raw honey to the bowl and mix everything together. Taste and add more honey if you like it a little sweeter.

* Please see the Resource section for recommended brands and their availability.

Ingredients

2-ounce package Eden Foods* arame seaweed
1 large carrot, shredded (about 1 cup)
1 cup green cabbage, shredded
½ cup red onion, thinly sliced
2 Tbsp tamari
3 Tbsp Eden Foods* toasted sesame oil
4 Tbsp Eden Foods* brown rice vinegar
1–2 Tbsp raw honey

Warm Arame Salad

Use the same ingredients as above, but remove the vinegar.

Soak the arame as above and strain. Sauté the vegetables in the sesame oil until soft and tender, about 6–7 minutes. Remove vegetables from heat and add in the arame, tamari, and honey. Mix well and serve warm.

Kale and Sweet Potato Salad

Makes 2 servings as a meal
Makes 4 servings as a side

Directions

Boil sweet potatoes, cool, and cut into bite-sized pieces.

In a large bowl, toss kale, maple syrup, and olive oil. Add the other ingredients except hemp seeds and mix well. Top with hemp seeds and serve.

Ingredients

- 2 cups raw kale, chopped
- 1 cup cooked garbanzo beans, drained, and cooled
- 1 large garlic clove, minced
- ½ red onion, thinly sliced
- 1 apple, cored, thinly sliced with skin
- 2 small- to medium-sized sweet potatoes
- 1 Tbsp real maple syrup
- 2 Tbsp hemp seeds
- 3 Tbsp extra virgin olive oil
- 1 Tbsp raw apple cider vinegar
- ½ tsp fresh ginger, grated
- ⅛ tsp unrefined salt
- ⅛ tsp crushed black pepper

What's in the Fridge Salad

Makes 6 servings

With permission from my dear friend Nicole Roberts, who writes:

This salad is my go-to salad. I could eat this salad every day, in fact, usually I do. My husband will ask me, "Hey, could you make that yummy salad?" What makes it a hit is the avocado and the dates. The two tastes combined make my heart happy. I hope you enjoy it as much as I do!

Directions

Put the ingredients in a giant bowl. Pour the olive oil evenly over the salad. Sprinkle the unrefined salt, powdered garlic, and onion on top. Toss and serve!

* Please see the Resource section for recommended brands and their availability.

Dressing

½ cup extra virgin olive oil
1 tsp powdered garlic
1 tsp powdered onion
Sprinkle of unrefined salt

Ingredients

3–4 cups of any lettuce (arugula, romaine, kale, mesclun mix, butter leaf, spinach, or a combination)
¼ red onion, diced
2–3 radishes with greens, sliced
2 scallions, diced
10 cherry tomatoes, halved
2–4 dates, pitted and cut in half
1 avocado, cubed
1 cup red cabbage, chopped
1–4 garlic cloves, minced

Optional Ingredients

2–4 figs, halved
Handful of raisins
1–2 dandelion leaves
10 grapes, halved
10 pitted Kalamata olives*
1 tsp capers
Handful of cashews

Arugula and Pear Salad with Feta

Makes 4 Servings

Directions

Place ingredients in a large bowl. Mix and serve.

Ingredients

2 cups fresh arugula
15 cherry tomatoes, halved
1 small red onion, chopped small
1 pear, cut into bite-sized pieces
½ cup crumbled feta cheese
¼ cup fresh cilantro or basil, chopped
½ cup broccoli sprouts
½ cup Mediterranean olives, pitted
2–3 Tbsp extra virgin olive oil
1 Tbsp hemp seed oil
1 Tbsp raw apple cider vinegar or coconut vinegar

Unrefined salt and black pepper to taste

Mediterranean Arugula Salad with Heirloom Tomatoes

Makes 2 servings as a main dish
Makes 4–6 servings as a side

Directions

Add arugula, tomatoes, onions, garlic, and olives in a large salad bowl and mix. Then add both oils, vinegar, salt, and pepper to taste. Top with fresh avocado and mix lightly without mashing the avocado. Serve.

* Please see the Resource section for recommended brands and their availability.

Ingredients

3 cups fresh arugula, small leaves or chopped
2 medium heirloom tomatoes, sliced
1 small red onion, diced
1 clove fresh garlic, minced
1 ripe avocado, sliced
7–10 Mediterranean olives
2 Tbsp hemp seed oil
3 Tbsp extra virgin olive oil
1 Tbsp Coconut Secret* coconut vinegar

Unrefined salt to taste
Black pepper to taste

High-Protein Kale Salad

Makes 4 Servings

Directions

Drain and discard liquid from garbanzo beans. Mix all ingredients well and enjoy!

* Please see the Resource section for recommended brands and their availability.

Ingredients

3 cups of fresh kale, chopped small
1 (15 ounce) can garbanzo beans*
3 cloves garlic, minced
1 cup Locatelli* Pecorino Romano sheep cheese, coarsely grated
2 Tbsp fresh dill
4 Tbsp extra virgin olive oil
2 Tbsp coconut vinegar

Unrefined salt to taste
Black pepper to taste

High-Protein Pasta Salad

Makes 6 Servings

Directions

Cook and cool the pasta. Add other ingredients to cooled pasta, toss, and serve. Or store in airtight container in refrigerator for up to 3 days.

* Please see the Resource section for recommended brands and their availability.

Ingredients

1 pound (2 boxes) Felicia* quinoa pasta
1 medium red onion, chopped small
2 cloves garlic, minced
1 celery stalk, chopped small
7–10 cherry tomatoes, halved
1 celery stalk, diced
7–10 Mediterranean olives, pitted
¼ cup fresh parsley, chopped
⅛ tsp powdered garlic
⅛ tsp powdered onion
½ cup extra virgin olive oil
2 Tbsp balsamic vinegar

Unrefined salt to taste
Black pepper to taste

High-Enzymatic Salad

Makes 4 Servings

Directions

In a large bowl mix all ingredients and serve.

* Please see the Resource section for recommended brands and their availability.

Ingredients

2 cups fresh arugula
15 cherry tomatoes, halved
1 small red onion, chopped small
1 celery stalk, chopped small
2–3 forkfuls of raw, lacto-fermented carrot ginger sauerkraut*
½ cup cooked and cooled garbanzo beans
2 radishes, sliced thin
¼ cup fresh cilantro or parsley, chopped
1 cup raw shiitake mushrooms, sliced thin, stems removed
½ cup broccoli sprouts
2–3 Tbsp extra virgin olive oil
1 Tbsp hemp seed oil
1 Tbsp raw apple cider vinegar or coconut vinegar
Unrefined salt to taste
Black pepper to taste

Creamy Ranch Dressing

Makes 8 Servings

Directions

Mix all ingredients well and refrigerate in a sealed container for up to seven days.

* Please see the Resource section for recommended brands and their availability.

Ingredients

1 cup Chosen Foods* avocado mayonnaise
½ cup Kalona* whole-milk sour cream
¼ cup fresh or dried oregano
¼ cup fresh parsley, chopped
¼ cup fresh chives, chopped
¼ cup fresh dill, chopped
⅛ tsp powdered onion
⅛ tsp powdered garlic
⅛ tsp unrefined salt
⅛ tsp black pepper

High-Antioxidant Salad Dressing

Makes 4 Servings

Directions

Mix all ingredients. Store ingredients in airtight container in the refrigerator for one week. This makes enough dressing for 4 cups of mixed salad ingredients. Store dressing in container separate from salad ingredients until ready to serve. Add to your favorite salad.

* Please see the Resource section for recommended brands and their availability.

Ingredients

½ cup extra virgin olive oil
¼ cup hemp seed oil
2 Tbsp Coconut Secret*raw coconut vinegar
Juice of ½ lemon or lime
⅛ tsp powdered onion
2 cloves fresh garlic, minced

Unrefined salt to taste
Black pepper to taste

Appetizers

Grandma Fran's Bruschetta	95
Grandma Fran's Pesto	97
Grandma Fran's Heavenly Italian Garlic Bread	99
Collard Green Spring Rolls	101
Cauliflower Pizza	103
Grandma Fran's Stuffed Mushrooms	105
Honey Lemon Asparagus with Slivered Almonds	107
Avocado Dip	107
Hummus	109
My Family's Thanksgiving Stuffing	110

Chapter **Eight**

Grandma Fran's Bruschetta

Makes 12–14 servings

Grandma loved to make bruschetta and we loved eating it.

Directions

Add all ingredients (except bread) in a large bowl and mix well. Add 1 tablespoon of mixture to each piece of bread and serve.

* Please see the Resource section for recommended brands and their availability.

Ingredients

8 Roma tomatoes, diced very small
½ yellow onion, minced small
2 cloves fresh garlic, minced small
⅓ cup fresh basil, minced fine
¼ cup fresh Locatelli* Pecorino Romano sheep cheese, grated
⅛ tsp powdered onion
⅛ tsp powdered garlic
⅛ tsp unrefined salt
½ tsp crushed black pepper
½ cup extra virgin olive oil
1 baguette or bread of choice from Shewolfbakery.com,* sliced into 1-inch thick slices

Grandma Fran's Pesto

Makes 8 Servings

When my sister and I were kids, we used to ask Grandma if she could make the green macaroni, and she knew exactly what she needed to do. Grandma would grind the basil in an old-fashioned hand grinder. Making Grandma's pesto keeps her memory alive in our hearts.

Directions

Place all the ingredients in a food processor or blender. Pulse to create a creamy, pourable, yet medium-thick consistency.

Top your favorite pasta or use it as a dip for healthy chips or fresh vegetables.

Note: Makes enough pesto for ½ pound of cooked pasta.

Ingredients

- **1 large bunch fresh basil leaves (about 2 cups), rinsed and dried**
- **3 medium cloves fresh garlic**
- **½ cup raw pine nuts**
- **¾ cup Parmesan cheese, freshly grated (preferably imported sheep cheese for traditional Italian flavor)**
- **3–4 Tbsp extra virgin olive oil**
- **Pinch of unrefined salt**
- **Black pepper to taste**

Grandma Fran's Heavenly Italian Garlic Bread

Makes 8 servings

Grandma would make the most delicious garlic bread you could ever dream of. Everyone would sit around the table and enjoy Grandma's hot-out-of-the-oven garlic bread and share a lot of laughs.

Directions

In a large bowl, add the yeast and water. Stir well to dissolve. Add the honey, olive oil, salt, and 2 cups of flour. Beat with an electric hand mixer on medium speed until blended. Then add in the last cup of flour and mix by hand to form a dough. Knead the dough for about 7–8 minutes and then place the dough in a medium bowl greased with olive oil. Rotate the dough as you place it in the bowl so all sides are covered in olive oil. Cover the dough with a dish towel and let sit for an hour in a warm place for the dough to rise. Bread should double in size.

Preheat oven to 375ºF. Remove risen dough from the bowl and place on baking sheet lined with parchment paper. Pound the dough down with your fist and cover with a dish towel for 30 minutes to let the dough rise again. Bake for 30 minutes or until lightly brown. Remove from the oven.

While it was still hot, Grandma would slice open the top, making a small well, and drizzle olive oil and fresh minced garlic, salt, and black pepper.

Follow the example of Grandma and then add fresh Italian Romano grated cheese. Place back in the oven for 5 more minutes and serve.

* Please see the Resource section for recommended brands and their availability.

Ingredients

3 cups all-purpose einkorn flour*
2 Tbsp extra virgin olive oil
1 tsp unrefined salt
1 tsp raw honey
¼ ounce Rapunzel* organic active dry yeast
2 cups warm water

Toppings

3 cloves fresh garlic, minced
½ cup extra virgin olive oil
1 cup fresh Locatelli* Pecorino Romano cheese, grated

Black pepper to taste
Unrefined salt to taste

Collard Green Spring Rolls

Makes 12 servings

Directions

In a medium bowl, add coconut teriyaki, sesame oil, raw honey, garlic, black pepper, scallions, and peanut butter. Whisk all ingredients and set aside.

Take one collard green at a time and lay it down flat on a cutting board and add fillings. Start with bean sprouts, cucumber, carrots, avocado, and the red bell pepper. Fold the collard green over so the vegetables are secure inside. Tuck in each side of the collard green and continue to roll until it appears as a spring roll. Arrange spring rolls on a plate and serve with the dipping sauce.

* Please see the Resource section for recommended brands and their availability.

Ingredients for Filling

12 raw collard greens, stems removed
3 medium carrots, peeled and thinly sliced vertically into 4-inch slices
2 cucumbers, peeled and thinly sliced vertically into 4-inch slices
2 red bell pepper, thinly sliced
2 ripe avocados, thinly sliced
1 cup bean sprouts

Ingredients for Sauce

½ cup Coconut Secret* coconut teriyaki
½ cup toasted sesame oil
¼ cup raw honey
1 Tbsp garlic, finely minced
½ cup raw wild jungle peanut butter
1 scallion, minced small
½ tsp fresh black pepper, crushed

Cauliflower Pizza

Makes 4 servings

This pizza is so yummy, I cannot wait for you to make it.

Directions

Preheat the oven to 375ºF. Remove the stems and leaves from the cauliflower and pull apart the florets. In a large pot, cover the cauliflower with 6 cups of water and boil the florets for 7 minutes. Drain the water and let the cauliflower cool for 10 minutes.

Place the cauliflower in a food processor and pulse until it looks like rice. Place the cauliflower *rice* in a cheesecloth or a dish towel and squeeze out the excess water into the sink. Now put your cauliflower *rice/dough* in a large bowl. Add the garlic, powdered onion, basil, parsley, oregano, egg or flaxseeds, salt, and pepper. Mix well with your hands.

Line a baking sheet with parchment paper and add the *dough* mixture, forming it into a round pizza pan and bake for 20 minutes. Then, add about ½ cup *Pomodoro* sauce to your cooked *crust*, leaving ½ inch from the ends dry. Add the veggies and cheese. Bake it again for about 5–7 minutes. Serve immediately with remaining ½ cup of *Pomodoro* sauce for dipping. Enjoy!

* Please see the Resource section for recommended brands and their availability.

Ingredients

2 heads of fresh cauliflower, approximately 3 pounds each
2 cloves fresh garlic, minced
1 tsp powdered onion
1 Tbsp fresh basil, finely chopped
1 tsp fresh parsley, finely chopped
½ tsp fresh oregano
Unrefined salt to taste
Black pepper to taste
1 Tbsp fresh ground flaxseeds
Or 1 egg
1 cup homemade *Pomodoro* sauce (page 129)
1 cup fresh mozzarella, sliced thin
1 cup mixed vegetables of choice
Such as: onions, broccoli florets, mushrooms, or spinach

Grandma Fran's Stuffed Mushrooms

Makes 24 mushrooms

During the holidays, I could not wait for Grandma's stuffed mushrooms. The aroma alone would capture us all. I will never forget the first time that Grandma showed me how to make her mushrooms. I was in shock that she would put the stems right back inside the mushroom. Till this day, I keep her holiday tradition alive by making her stuffed mushrooms. Everyone in my family literally fights over them, so I must be sure that I prepare enough. Now, get your apron on and let's start stuffing mushrooms.

Directions

Preheat oven to 350ºF. Wash mushrooms and dry them well. Remove all the stems. Place mushroom caps, gill side up, in a large baking pan.

Crumble half the stems into a bowl, discarding the remaining stems. In a separate large mixing bowl, add breadcrumbs, cream cheese, grated cheese, basil, parsley, salt, pepper, garlic, powdered onion, and olive oil. Mix well for a thick consistency. Combine the mushroom stems into the cream cheese mixture and mix well.

Add water and the butter to bottom of the baking dish. Spoon about 1 tablespoon of the filling into each mushroom cap. Mix the toppings in a bowl and add ½ teaspoon of the mixture to the tops of each stuffed mushroom. Bake for 30 minutes and enjoy!

* Please see the Resource section for recommended brands and their availability.

Ingredients

24 large stuffing mushrooms
Two 8-ounce containers Organic Valley* cream cheese
Or two 8-ounce containers Kite Hill* plain cream cheese
½ cup Watusee* chickpea breadcrumbs
½ cup extra virgin olive oil
1 cup Locatelli* Pecorino Romano sheep cheese, grated
¼ cup fresh basil, minced
¼ cup fresh parsley, minced
¼ cup fresh garlic, minced
1 tsp powdered onion
⅛ tsp fresh ground black pepper
1 cup filtered water
½ stick unsalted butter, cubed

Unrefined salt to taste

Toppings

¼ cup Watusee* chickpea breadcrumbs
¼ cup Locatelli* Pecorino Romano sheep cheese, grated
1 Tbsp extra virgin olive oil

Honey Lemon Asparagus with Slivered Almonds

Makes 4 servings

Directions

In a large stainless skillet, add coconut oil and heat on medium heat. Add the garlic, salt, and pepper and sauté until lightly brown. Now, add the almonds, honey, and lemon, blending into the garlic. Then, add the asparagus and scallions. Cover and cook for about 7 minutes, stirring every 2–3 minutes so it doesn't stick. Asparagus should still have a crunch and not be mushy or soft. Add extra cilantro or parsley, salt, and pepper. Replace lid and let sit for one minute. Serve.

Ingredients

1 pound fresh asparagus, cleaned and cut in half, ends removed
2 cloves fresh garlic, minced
2 scallions, chopped small
1 Tbsp raw honey
½ cup slivered almonds
Juice of 1 fresh lemon
1 Tbsp extra virgin coconut oil
Unrefined salt to taste
Black pepper to taste
⅛ cup fresh cilantro or parsley, chopped

Avocado Dip

Makes 6 Servings

Directions

Mix well and serve.

Ingredients

3 ripe avocados, mashed
Juice of 1 fresh lime or lemon
1 tsp extra virgin olive oil
¼ tsp garlic powder
¼ tsp onion powder
¼ cup fresh cilantro, chopped

Unrefined salt to taste
Black pepper to taste

Hummus

Makes 4-6 servings

Directions

Drain and rinse garbanzo beans. Then add all the ingredients to blender or food processor and blend for 3–5 minutes on low until thoroughly mixed and smooth. Garnish with fresh cilantro or parsley (optional).

Ingredients

16-ounce can of plain garbanzo beans in water
2 Tbsp fresh lemon juice
1½ Tbsp raw tahini
2 cloves garlic, minced
½ tsp unrefined salt
⅛ tsp powdered onion
2 Tbsp extra virgin olive oil
1 Tbsp fresh cilantro or parsley, chopped (optional)

Health Tip

Choose a home-cooked meal of real food instead of a fast-food-chain meal.

My Family's Thanksgiving Stuffing

Makes 8–10 servings

Directions

Preheat oven to 350ºF. Prepare the rice, following the instructions on the package. In a large stainless skillet on medium heat, add the butter and red palm oil. Add the onions, garlic, salt, and pepper. Sauté until lightly brown. Next, add the celery, mushrooms, powdered garlic and onion, and mix. Cook for 5–7 minutes. Add the cooked rice and mix well. Add the grated cheese, chicken broth, basil, oregano, parsley, and mix. Cover and cook on low to medium heat for 15 minutes, stirring frequently.

Place the mixture in a 9x13 baking pan and bake for 30 minutes. Serve as a wonderful addition to your Thanksgiving meal.

* Please see the Resource section for recommended brands and their availability.

Ingredients

- 2 cups cooked Truroots* germinated brown rice
- 1½ cups organic Imagine Foods* free range chicken broth
- 1 small yellow onion, chopped small
- 2 cloves fresh garlic, chopped small
- 2 stalks celery, diced
- 10 cremini mushrooms, chopped
- ½ cup (1 stick) unsalted butter
- 1 tsp fresh oregano, finely chopped
- 2 Tbsp fresh basil, finely chopped
- 2 Tbsp fresh parsley, finely chopped
- 1 tsp powdered garlic
- 1 tsp powdered onion
- 1 Tbsp red palm oil
- 1 cup Stella* organic Parmesan cheese, shredded

Black pepper to taste
Unrefined salt to taste

Health Tip

Choose raw, jungle peanuts over regular peanuts. Regular peanuts may contain aflatoxins or mold that increase allergies and other health issues. Jungle peanuts are the original peanut and a nutrient-dense food that does not contain these carcinogenic compounds. Choosing them will have a positive impact on your health *and* the environment.

Dinner

Wild Alaskan Sockeye Salmon Teriyaki	113
Raw Vegan Fettuccine Alfredo	115
Homemade Meatballs	117
Grandma Fran's Sicilian Baked Macaroni	119
Creamy Kamut Pasta with Chicken and Broccoli	121
Delicious Chicken Chili	123
Cream of Mushroom Crock Pot Chicken	124
Pasta Bolognese	125
Grandma Fran's *Pasta e Piselli*	127
Italian Pomodoro with Pasta	129
Cauliflower Fried Rice	131
Red Lentil Pasta Alfredo with Broccoli	133
Mouth-Watering Chicken Franchese	135
Zucchini Pasta Italiano	137
Amazingly Delicious and Creamy Red Lentil Pasta Pesto	139
Vegetarian Chili	141
Pasta Che Non Basta	143
Vegetarian Thai Cuisine in Seven Easy Steps	144
Grandma Fran's Italian Style Zucchini	146
Tri-Color Quinoa Pilaf	147
High-Antioxidant Red Lentil Pasta	148
Zucchini Noodles with Creamy Walnut Pesto	149
Beef Chili	150

Chapter

Nine

Wild Alaskan Sockeye Salmon Teriyaki

Makes 6 servings

Directions

Preheat oven to 350ºF.

Place salmon in a large bowl and set aside. In another bowl, add all other ingredients and mix well. Add sauce over the 6 salmon pieces, cover and marinate in refrigerator for 4–6 hours or overnight.

Place marinated salmon pieces in a baking pan greased with coconut oil and bake for 20 minutes. Serve with a salad, raw ginger carrot sauerkraut, and/or *Lemon Honey Asparagus with Almonds* (see page 129).

* Please see the Resource section for recommended brands and their availability.

Ingredients

- 2 pounds fresh, wild sockeye salmon, filleted, cleaned, and cut into 6 pieces
- 2 cloves fresh garlic, minced
- ½ cup Coconut Secret* coconut teriyaki sauce
- 1 Tbsp extra virgin coconut oil
- ½ tsp powdered ginger
- ½ tsp black pepper
- ½ tsp unrefined salt
- 1 Tbsp raw honey
- ½ cup toasted sesame oil

Health Tip

Wild salmon contains much higher levels of omega-3 than its farmed counterpart. So, please choose wild over farmed for its many benefits as described in Chapter Eleven entitled, "Farmed and Dangerous" in *Stop Battling Disease & Start Building Wellness*.

Raw Vegan Fettuccine Alfredo

Makes 2 servings

With permission from my dear friend, Lisa Love (Pupo):
I was so inspired to create this recipe because I am a lover of health and nutrition! I love to take comfort foods and make them as healthy as possible. Remember the saying: Let food be thy medicine, and medicine be thy food!

Directions

Spiralize 3½ zucchini and save the other half zucchini for blending in sauce.

Place spiralized zucchini in large bowl, sprinkle with a pinch of salt and set aside.

In a blender or food processor, blend all the rest of ingredients including salt, adding the water slowly, keeping a very thick consistency. The water content in spiralized zucchini will naturally thin the sauce. You may not need all the water. Mix the sauce with spiralized zucchini, toss, and serve.

Note:

For a cooked version, you can boil water and place the zucchini noodles in it for a few minutes to warm. Drain thoroughly before adding sauce. Toss and serve.

Ingredients

4 medium zucchini with peel
1 cup raw cashews
¼ cup Bob's Red Mill nutritional yeast *
Juice of ½ lemon
½ cup distilled water
1 tsp Coconut Secret* coconut aminos
⅛ tsp powdered nutmeg

Black pepper to taste
Unrefined salt to taste

* Please see the Resource section for recommended brands and their availability.

Homemade Meatballs

Makes 16 meatballs

Directions

In a large bowl, mix ground beef, eggs, *Pomodoro* sauce, salt, and pepper. Add onions, garlic, cheese, basil, parsley and oregano and mix well.

Roll the meatball mixture into balls about 1 inch in diameter. Place meatballs on a dish and set aside. Heat a large stainless skillet with 1 tablespoon red palm oil on medium heat. Cook meatballs for about 12 minutes, turning frequently. Enjoy as is or add to a pan of *Pomodoro* sauce and cook for 30 minutes and serve over pasta of choice.

* Please see the Resource section for recommended brands and their availability.

Ingredients

1½ pounds ground beef
2 large eggs
1 medium yellow onion, diced small
2 cloves garlic, minced
½ cup fresh basil, chopped
¼ cup fresh parsley, chopped
1 tsp ground or fresh oregano
1 cup fresh Locatelli* Pecorino Romano sheep cheese, grated
⅛ tsp unrefined salt
½ tsp black pepper
1 Tbsp red palm oil
2 Tbsp leftover homemade *Pomodoro* sauce (see page 129)

Grandma Fran's Sicilian Baked Macaroni

Makes 10 servings

I love eggplants. They're not only loaded with minerals, such as phosphorus, copper, thiamine, zinc, niacin, magnesium, and selenium, but they taste great. Eggplants were a staple in our Italian household. Every New Year's Eve Day, Grandma would fry eggplant all morning and then place it on paper bags to drain off the oil. She would prepare her recipe that was passed all the way down from her great-grandmother.

We wouldn't eat this until New Year's Day, so the flavors would all come together as Grandma had explained. My precious, daughter, Michaela, was only six years old when Big Grandma went to be with the Lord at the age of ninety-three. Big Grandma is the name Michaela gave her great-grandmother. Although Michaela's memories of Big Grandma are fading, she remembers Grandma's Sicilian Baked Macaroni. The essence of Big Grandma's love remains in her heart forever.

Directions

Preheat oven to 350ºF. Remove ends from each eggplant. Remove the skin lengthwise in a striped pattern, so it is like a zebra pattern. Slice vertically into slabs about ¼ thick. Pile the sliced eggplant onto a plate and set aside. Heat a large stainless skillet and add extra virgin olive oil. Cook eggplant in hot oil for about 2 minutes on each side and repeat process until all eggplant is done.

Place each piece of cooked eggplant on a plate that's covered with paper towels to remove some of the oil. Layer the eggplant and paper towels. You can also follow Grandma's practice and use good old brown paper bags.

Ingredients

2 large eggplants
6 cups of *Pasta Bolognese* sauce, (recipe on page 125)
2 pounds Felicia's* gluten-free mezzi rigatoni mais-riso
½ cup fresh basil, chopped
2 pounds Maplebrook Farm* fresh mozzarella, sliced medium thin
1 cup Locatelli* Pecorino Romano sheep cheese, grated

Grandma Fran's Sicilian Baked Macaroni (Con't)

Cook pasta for only half the time the directions require. Drain and place pasta in a large pasta bowl. Add enough Bolognese sauce to wet the pasta, so it doesn't stick. Set aside. In a ziti pan large enough to fit 2 pounds pasta, add a small amount of Bolognese, just enough to cover the bottom.

Add ¾ pounds pasta to the pan and add more Bolognese. Then add enough eggplant to cover the pasta. Generously add grated cheese and mozzarella. Repeat this process until you have three layers and all the ingredients are used. Add the grated cheese and fresh basil to the top layer and bake in the oven for 35–40 minutes. Allow to cool for 20 minutes before serving, because the macaroni will break apart.

* Please see the Resource section for recommended brands and their availability.

Creamy Kamut Pasta with Chicken and Broccoli

Makes 4 servings

Directions

Follow cooking directions for pasta.

Add coconut oil and butter to medium-sized, stainless saucepan. Sauté onions, garlic, and mushrooms on medium heat until lightly brown, adding salt and pepper to taste. Add diced chicken breasts and cook until golden brown and no longer pink in the middle. Add heavy cream and grated cheese. Stir well and reduce heat. Cover and simmer for 5 minutes.

Add steamed broccoli and basil. Mix well, add to pasta, and serve.

* Please see the Resource section for recommended brands and their availability.

Ingredients

12-ounce box Eden* kamut pasta
1 stick unsalted butter
1 cup heavy cream
2 pasture-raised, boneless chicken breasts, cut into bite-sized pieces
2 cups broccoli florets, lightly steamed
2 cups cremini mushrooms, diced
1 Tbsp extra virgin coconut oil
2 cloves fresh garlic, minced
1 small onion, diced small
¼ cup fresh basil, chopped
1 cup Locatelli* Pecorino Romano sheep cheese, grated

Black pepper to taste
Unrefined salt to taste

Delicious Chicken Chili

Makes 6–8 servings

Directions

On medium heat, place extra virgin coconut oil in medium-sized stainless pot. Add chicken and cook thoroughly. Add onion, garlic, red and green peppers, cremini mushrooms, and cilantro.

As this is simmering add the black pepper, cumin powder, unrefined salt, turmeric powder, garlic powder, onion powder, bay leaves, chickpeas, and tomatoes. Mix well. Simmer for 40 minutes or until fully cooked. Top with sour cream and fresh avocado.

* Please see the Resource section for recommended brands and their availability.

Ingredients

1 generous Tbsp extra virgin coconut oil
6 boneless chicken breasts, cut into bite-sized strips
1 medium onion, diced
4 cloves garlic, minced
1 medium red pepper, diced
1 medium green pepper, diced
1 cup cremini mushrooms, sliced
1 bunch cilantro, chopped
1 tsp black pepper
1½ tsp cumin powder
1½ tsp unrefined salt
1 tsp turmeric powder
1 Tbsp garlic powder
1 tsp onion powder
4 large bay leaves
1 cup cooked chickpeas
2 cups tomatoes, diced

Toppings

Kalona* sour cream
Fresh avocado, diced

Cream of Mushroom Crock Pot Chicken

Makes 4 servings

Directions

Add all ingredients to crock pot. Cook on low for 6–8 hours. Serve with either quinoa or brown rice.

* Please see the Resource section for recommended brands and their availability.

Ingredients

1 Tbsp coconut oil
½ cup (1 stick) unsalted butter
4 boneless chicken breasts, diced into bite-sized pieces
25 cremini or baby portabella mushrooms, halved
2 cups heavy cream*
2 cups fresh broccoli florets
1 Tbsp powdered garlic
1 Tbsp powdered onion

Unrefined salt to taste
Black pepper to taste

Pasta Bolognese

Makes 4 servings

Top your favorite pasta with my delicious Bolognese sauce.

Directions

Add olive oil to large stainless pot and allow to heat on low to medium heat for 1 minute. Add onions, salt, and pepper. Sauté for about 1 minute. Add garlic and sauté for another minute. Add the ground beef. Allow beef to cook for about 10 minutes or until it becomes brown, stirring every 3–4 minutes.

When beef is browned, add crushed tomatoes, stirring well to mix ingredients. Add the onion, garlic, and fresh herbs. Mix well. Allow to simmer on low heat with lid half on for a total of 40 minutes, stirring every 5–7 minutes.

While sauce is simmering, cook pasta as directed on package. When sauce is finished, add to pasta, mix well, and serve with grated cheese.

* Please see the Resource section for recommended brands and their availability.

Ingredients

2 pounds grass-fed ground beef
1 medium yellow onion, diced
3 cloves garlic, minced
¼ cup fresh parsley, chopped
7–8 fresh basil leaves, chopped
1 sprig fresh oregano, chopped
½ tsp powdered onion
½ tsp powdered garlic
Six 18.3-ounce jars of Jovial* crushed tomatoes
3 Tbsp extra virgin olive oil
1 pound Felicia's* multigrain tortiglioni pasta

Unrefined salt to taste
Black pepper to taste

Topping:

Locatelli Percorino Romano sheep cheese, grated

Grandma Fran's *Pasta e Piselli*
(Pasta with Peas)

Makes 4 servings

Pasta with peas was a very simple, delicious comfort meal in our home. I knew as soon as I smelled the aroma of sautéed onions, Pasta with Peas were "what's for dinner."

Here is my healthy conversion of Grandma Fran's Pasta with Peas.

Directions

Cook pasta, following directions on package. While pasta is cooking, chop mushrooms, onion, basil, and oregano and set aside. Mince garlic and set aside.

In a large stainless pan on medium heat, add oil. Add onions, salt, and pepper and sauté for 3 minutes. Add mushrooms and peas. Mix well and cook an additional 7 minutes, stirring frequently. When the pasta is cooked (and before you drain pasta), add two full ladles of the hot pasta water into the peas, mixing it in. Then, drain the pasta. Add pasta to vegetable mixture, mix well, and remove from heat. Add fresh raw garlic, basil, and oregano. Mix well, then top with freshly grated cheese and serve.

I can almost see Grandma in the kitchen.

Ingredients

- 1 pound Truroots* ancient grain pasta penne
- 1 small yellow onion, chopped small
- 2–3 cloves, garlic, minced *(I love garlic so I always add extra)*
- ¼ cup fresh basil leaves, chopped
- 1 sprig fresh oregano, chopped
- 16-ounce bag frozen sweet peas
- 1 cup cremini mushrooms, chopped
- 2 Tbsp red palm oil or extra virgin coconut oil
- Unrefined salt to taste
- Black pepper to taste
- ½ cup Locatelli* Pecorino Romano sheep cheese, grated

* Please see the Resource section for recommended brands and their availability.

Italian Pomodoro with Pasta

Makes 4 servings

Directions

Prepare pasta according to package instructions.

In a medium stainless steel pot, add the coconut oil on low heat and allow oil to melt. Add sliced onion and minced garlic and sauté until lightly brown. Add salt and black pepper to taste.

When onion and garlic are lightly browned, stir in all diced tomatoes. Add basil leaves, oregano, parsley, garlic, onion, and stir. Cook on medium heat for 20 minutes, stirring occasionally.

Add feta cheese to hot, cooked pasta and mix well. Add sauce and top with grated cheese.

* Please see the Resource section for recommended brands and their availability.

Ingredients

1 Tbsp extra virgin coconut oil
Two 18.3-ounce jars Jovial* diced tomatoes
1 medium onion, thinly sliced
2 cloves garlic, minced
6–8 fresh basil leaves, chopped
2 sprigs fresh oregano, chopped
¼ cup fresh parsley, chopped
2 Tbsp coconut oil or red palm oil
½ tsp powdered onion
½ tsp powdered garlic
1 (8 ounce) container Organic Valley* crumbled feta
1 pound pasta* (your choice)

Unrefined salt to taste
Black pepper to taste

Topping:

Locatelli Percorino Romano cheese, grated

Cauliflower Fried Rice

Makes 2 servings as a meal
Makes 4 servings as a side

Directions

Cut the cauliflower into 5 or 6 sections, remove and discard stems. Put 4–5 florets in food processor and pulse until cauliflower begins to resemble rice. Remove from food processor, add to a bowl, and set aside. Repeat process until the entire head of cauliflower resembles rice.

In a large stainless skillet, add the butter or coconut oil and heat on medium to melt and evenly distribute. Add chopped onions, salt, and pepper, sautéing until lightly browned. Add the garlic and sauté for 1 minute. Add mushrooms and sauté for 3–4 minutes. Add the cauliflower rice, peas, carrots, and corn. Mix well.

Cover and cook for about 7 minutes, stirring every 2–3 minutes. After 7 minutes, add ½ cup of the coconut teriyaki and mix well. Cover.

When all veggies are fully cooked, after approximately 20 minutes, add the other ½ cup coconut teriyaki, scallions, and parsley. Mix, remove from heat, and serve.

Ingredients

1 large head cauliflower
2 cups frozen mixed peas, carrots, and corn
1 medium onion, diced small
2 scallions, chopped small
2 cloves garlic, minced small
1 cup baby portabella mushrooms, coarsely chopped
¼ cup fresh parsley, chopped
3 Tbsp butter
Or 3 Tbsp ghee or coconut oil
1 cup Coconut Secret* coconut teriyaki sauce

Unrefined salt to taste
Black pepper to taste

* Please see the Resource section for recommended brands and their availability.

Red Lentil Pasta Alfredo with Broccoli

Makes 4–6 servings

When I picked up my daughter Michaela from college for spring break, the first thing she requested was that I make her Mama's Alfredo with broccoli.

Directions

Lightly steam the broccoli florets.

In a large stainless pot, cook red lentil pasta according to package directions.

While the pasta is cooking, add the extra virgin coconut oil or red palm oil to a medium stainless pot. Allow to melt on medium heat and add the chopped onions, minced garlic, salt, and pepper. Sauté until lightly brown. Reduce the heat and add the cream and cheese, stirring every 2–3 minutes for a total of 10 minutes. When the alfredo comes to a light boil, remove from heat. Add broccoli and basil.

Top the red lentil pasta with this wonderful alfredo. Add grated cheese and serve.

* Please see the Resource section for recommended brands and their availability.

Ingredients

2 Tbsp extra virgin coconut oil or red palm oil
1 medium onion, chopped small
3 cloves garlic, minced
8 ounces Locatelli* Pecorino Romano sheep cheese, grated
2 cups raw dairy heavy cream or coconut cream*
2 cups fresh broccoli florets
6–8 leaves fresh basil, chopped small
1 pound red lentil pasta*

Unrefined salt to taste
Black pepper to taste

Mouth-Watering Chicken Franchese

Makes 4 servings

Directions

In medium bowl, place flour, salt, pepper, powdered garlic, and powdered onion. Mix well. In another bowl, beat the eggs. Coat the chicken with flour and then dip in the eggs and dip again in the flour.

In large stainless skillet, melt ½ cup (1 stick) of the butter over medium heat. Cook the chicken in the butter for about 6 minutes on each side, turning once, until no longer pink in center. Remove the chicken from skillet and add to a plate, cover to keep warm, and set aside.

Add remaining butter to hot skillet. Add the juice of one lemon and 1 tablespoon flour. Mix well. Return chicken to skillet and heat on both sides, allowing chicken to become coated with lemon-butter sauce. Add minced garlic, fresh parsley, and lemon slices to cover most of the chicken. Cover with lid and remove from heat. Serve with a salad and or a side of pasta.

Ingredients

Four 6-ounce boneless chicken breasts, thinly cut and tenderized*
3 eggs, beaten
1½ cups all-purpose einkorn flour*
1 tsp powdered garlic
1 tsp powdered onion
¾ cup (1½ sticks) unsalted butter
2 cloves fresh garlic, minced
Juice of 1 fresh lemon
¼ cup fresh parsley, chopped
1 additional lemon, sliced thin for garnish

Unrefined salt to taste
Black pepper to taste

*How to tenderize chicken breast:
Wrap one piece of boneless breast in plastic wrap. Place chicken in plastic on cutting board and either roll with rolling pin on both sides using pressure, or pound both sides several times with meat tenderizer. Remove from plastic and follow the recipe.

* Please see the Resource section for recommended brands and their availability.

Zucchini Pasta Italiano

Makes 4 servings

As a vegetarian, I consume a ton of fresh fruits and vegetables. So, when I think pasta, I think more veggies!

Directions

Push zucchini through a spiralizer until you fill up a large pasta bowl with your zucchini noodles. Add ½ teaspoon of salt, toss, and set aside.

In a large bowl, add tomatoes, garlic, basil, oregano, oil, and salt and pepper to taste. Mix well and add the contents to your "pasta." Mix well. Top with fresh grated cheese of your choice and serve.

My family are big cheese lovers so we also add shredded mozzarella cheese.

I guarantee this will be a hit in your home. Bon appétit!

Ingredients

- **12 medium-sized zucchini or yellow squash (approximately 3–4 zucchini per person)**
- **2 cups heirloom cherry tomatoes, halved**
- **4–6 cloves fresh garlic, minced**
- **12–14 fresh basil leaves, chopped small**
- **1 Tbsp fresh oregano**
- **4 Tbsp extra virgin olive oil**

Unrefined salt to taste
Black pepper to taste

Topping

Freshly grated cheese

Amazingly Delicious and Creamy Red Lentil Pasta Pesto

Makes 4 servings

Directions

Cook red lentil pasta according to the package directions. Set aside.

In a food processor, add and pulse basil, garlic, and pine nuts until coarsely chopped. Add ½ cup olive oil and process until smooth. Add salt and pepper to taste.

Add pesto to pasta. Mix well. Add coconut cream and mix well. Add 1 cup of cheese and serve.

I prefer Pecorino Romano sheep cheese.

* Please see the Resource section for recommended brands and their availability.

Ingredients

2 boxes of Felicia's* red lentil ziti pasta
4 cups fresh basil leaves, packed
3 cloves garlic
½ cup raw pignoli nuts a.k.a. pine nuts
½ cup extra virgin olive oil
1 cup Locatelli* Pecorino Romano sheep cheese, freshly grated (or cheese of choice)
2 cups full-fat coconut cream

Unrefined salt to taste
Freshly ground black pepper to taste

Vegetarian Chili

Makes 8–10 servings

Directions

In a large stainless pot, add coconut or red palm oil and cook on medium heat. Add onions, garlic, red pepper, salt, and pepper. Sauté until golden brown. Add tomatoes and beans. Mix well. Add the herbs, including cilantro and parsley, mix well again. Cover, lower heat to medium low, and cook for 35–40 minutes, stirring about every 5 minutes so the chili doesn't stick. Add toppings and serve.

* Please see the Resource section for recommended brands and their availability.

Ingredients

3 cups black beans, cooked (canned beans should be drained and rinsed)
1 cup kidney beans, cooked (canned beans should be drained and rinsed)
3 cloves garlic, minced
1 medium yellow onion, chopped small
Two 18.3-ounce jars Jovial* diced tomatoes
½ cup fresh cilantro, chopped
½ cup fresh parsley, chopped
1 red bell pepper, diced
1 Tbsp powdered turmeric, freshly ground
1 Tbsp powdered cumin
1 tsp powdered garlic
1 tsp powdered onion
2 Tbsp extra virgin coconut oil or red palm oil
1½ tsp unrefined salt
1½ tsp black pepper

Toppings

1 cup shredded raw cheddar cheese Or any non-dairy cheese from Kite Hill*
1 cup Kite Hill* sour cream
1 cup onion, thinly sliced

Pasta Che Non Basta

Pasta That's not Enough! (translation)

Makes 4 servings

With permission from my mother Adrienne, Grandma Fran's daughter.

This recipe is one of my favorite meals that my mom, Frances, would make in the summer when we would have an abundance of fresh tomatoes from the garden. I remember the beautiful scent of fresh basil.

Directions

In a large bowl, combine tomatoes, fresh basil, garlic, extra virgin olive oil, salt, and black pepper. Mix all ingredients together and let sit so that all the delicious flavors blend together.

Cook pasta according to package directions.

I prefer my pasta to be al dente, which means a bit firm yet not undercooked.

Then, drain your pasta, leaving just a drop of water. Add the tomato/basil mixture to the hot pasta, gently mixing, covering all the pasta. Add fresh grated Romano and fresh mozzarella.

This dish is so delicious it was named "pasta that's not enough" because you just can't stop eating it!

Bon appétit!

Ingredients

Felicia's* gluten-free multigrain tortiglioni
6 medium ripe tomatoes, diced
1 cup fresh basil leaves, chopped
4 large cloves fresh garlic, chopped
½ cup extra virgin olive oil
1 cup Locatelli* Pecorino Romano sheep cheese, freshly grated
1 cup fresh mozzarella, shredded

Unrefined salt to taste
Black pepper to taste

* Please see the Resource section for recommended brands and their availability.

Vegetarian Thai Cuisine in Seven Easy Steps

Makes 6 Servings

Ingredients

2 cups brown rice
2 Tbsp wild raw jungle peanut butter*
Juice of ½ lime
6 Tbsp Coconut Secret* coconut teriyaki
1 tsp dried or fresh ground turmeric
2 Tbsp toasted sesame oil
½ tsp powdered garlic
1 tsp ginger, freshly grated
½ tsp powdered onion
2 Tbsp raw honey or coconut sugar
½ cup plus 4 Tbsp coconut heavy cream
2 Tbsp extra virgin coconut oil or red palm oil
1 small onion, diced small
1 garlic clove, minced
Unrefined salt to taste
Black pepper to taste
1 cup raw string beans, cut in half
2 cups raw broccoli florets
1 cup bok choy, chopped small
½ cup raw carrots, thinly sliced
1 cup raw zucchini, cut into ¼-inch slices
1 cup sweet potatoes, diced small with or without skin, cooked until tender
½ cup red bell pepper, diced
1 cup Asian eggplant, cubed into ½-inch pieces
1 cup shiitake mushrooms, halved, without stems
6–8 fresh basil leaves, chopped small
½ cup jungle peanuts
¼ cup fresh cilantro, chopped
1 cup fresh bean sprouts
1 Tbsp red pepper flakes for sauce (optional)
Parsley (garnish)

Directions

Step 1. Cook brown rice by following directions on package. When fully cooked, cover and set aside, keeping it warm on the stove.

Step 2. In a medium bowl, add raw jungle peanut butter, juice of ½ lime, coconut teriyaki, turmeric, sesame oil, powdered garlic, ginger, powdered onion, coconut sugar or raw honey, and coconut cream. Whisk until everything is combined. Set aside.

Step 3. In a large stainless skillet, add coconut or red palm oil on medium heat and allow to melt, evenly distributing the oil.

Step 4. Add onions, garlic, peanuts, salt, and pepper, sautéing until lightly brown. Add all the vegetables except for the sprouts. Stir the vegetables every 2–3 minutes for a total of 10 minutes. Add more salt and pepper to taste.

Step 5. Add sauce, basil, cilantro, and bean sprouts on top of vegetables and mix well. Remove from heat and cover.

Step 6. Add the cooked rice to a plate and top with vegetables. Serve with a garnish of fresh parsley.

Step 7. Enjoy with family and friends.

* Please see the Resource section for recommended brands and their availability.

Grandma Fran's Italian Style Zucchini

Makes 6 servings

This recipe has been in my Italian family for decades and I want to share this with you.

Directions

In a large stainless skillet, add the olive oil on low heat. Then, add garlic, onion, and salt and pepper to taste. Sauté on low heat for 2–3 minutes. Add zucchini and sauté on low heat for 2–3 minutes. Add tomatoes, basil, and parsley. Mix well. Cover and simmer on low heat for 20 minutes, stirring about every 4–5 minutes. After 20 minutes, the zucchini should be fully cooked. Remove from heat and add the freshly grated cheese. Allow cheese to melt and serve.

Grandma would always add just a little bit more cheese to everyone's dish.

I suggest Locatelli Pecorino Romano. This is grass-fed sheep cheese for exceptional authentic Italian flavor. This can be added to your favorite pasta or as a side dish to complement any meal. Guaranteed to make your house smell like a town in Italy and a great way to get the whole family to eat veggies. Bon appétit!

Ingredients

- 4–5 medium-sized fresh zucchini, cut into ¼-inch pieces with skin
- One 18.3-ounce jar of Jovial* diced tomatoes
- 3 cloves fresh garlic, minced
- 8–10 fresh basil leaves, chopped small
- ¼ cup fresh parsley, chopped small
- 1 small onion, chopped small
- 4–6 Tbsp fresh Locatelli* Pecorino Romano sheep cheese, coarsely grated
- 3 Tbsp extra virgin olive oil

Unrefined salt to taste
Black pepper to taste

* Please see the Resource section for recommended brands and their availability.

Tri-Color Quinoa Pilaf

Makes 4 servings as a side
Makes 1 serving as a meal

Quinoa is a complete protein and it is plant based.

Directions

Use a medium-sized stainless saucepan to cook the quinoa according to directions on the package.

Using a large stainless steel skillet with a lid, add coconut oil, celery, onion, garlic, carrots, mushrooms, and salt. Sauté until soft. Cover and cook for about 10 minutes and then add the frozen sweet peas. Cook additional 5 minutes. Add the quinoa and mix well. Cook for another 10 minutes, stirring occasionally. Add the cilantro, pine nuts, and lime juice. Mix well. If needed, add additional salt.

Serve with love and enjoy!

* Please see the Resource section for recommended brands and their availability.

Ingredients

1 cup uncooked quinoa*
1 Tbsp extra virgin coconut oil
2 stalks celery, diced
1 medium yellow onion, diced small
3 cloves garlic, minced
2 carrots, shredded
1 cup medium-sized shiitake mushrooms, chopped without stems
1 (10 ounce) bag frozen sweet peas
½ cup pine nuts
¼ cup fresh cilantro or parsley, chopped
Juice of 1 fresh lime

Unrefined salt to taste

High-Antioxidant Red Lentil Pasta

Makes 4–6 servings

Directions

Cook pasta following the directions on the box.

In a medium bowl, add avocados, garlic, olive oil, coconut teriyaki, tahini, salt, and pepper. Mix well. Add to pasta and mix.

Add all other vegetables to pasta, mix and top each dish with ¼ cup of your choice of sprouts and serve.

I like to top this dish with watercress sprouts, bean sprouts, alfalfa sprouts or pea sprouts.

Enjoy!

* Please see the Resource section for recommended brands and their availability.

Ingredients

1 pound red lentil pasta (2 eight-ounce boxes)
2 Tbsp raw tahini
2 ripe avocados, diced
¼ cup plus 1 Tbsp Coconut Secret* coconut teriyaki
4 Tbsp extra virgin olive oil
3 cloves garlic, minced
1 small onion, chopped small
4 raw asparagus spears, chopped into ½-inch pieces
2 medium tomatoes, diced
¼ cup fresh cilantro, chopped small

Unrefined salt to taste
Black pepper to taste

1–2 cups sprouts of choice

Zucchini Noodles with Creamy Walnut Pesto

Makes 4 servings

OMG, this is sooo good!

Directions

Push zucchini through a spiralizer and set aside. Add the rest of the ingredients into a food processor. Pulse on high for 3 minutes, then remove. Add to zucchini noodles and toss well. Add your favorite grated cheese.

Yummo!

Ingredients

12 medium zucchini
½ cup extra virgin olive oil
2 cloves garlic
½ cup raw walnuts
2 avocados
2 medium tomatoes, diced
6 fresh basil leaves
1 sprig fresh oregano
¼ cup fresh parsley
1 apple, peeled, cored, and diced
⅛ tsp powdered onion

Unrefined salt to taste
Black pepper to taste

Grated cheese of choice

Health Tip

If you're a meat eater, take a pass on the drugged-up, hormone-laden factory-farmed meat and eggs. Instead, choose grass fed and pasture raised.

Beef Chili

Makes 8–10 Servings

Directions

In a large stainless pot, add coconut or red palm oil and heat on medium heat. Add onions, garlic, red pepper, salt, and pepper. Sauté until golden brown. Add ground beef and cook until brown. Add tomatoes, beans, the herbs—including cilantro and parsley—and mix. Cover and lower the heat to medium low and cook for 35–40 minutes, stirring about every 5 minutes so chili doesn't stick. Add toppings and serve.

* Please see the Resource section for recommended brands and their availability.

Ingredients

2 pounds grass-fed ground beef
1 cup black beans, cooked (canned beans should be drained and rinsed)
3 cloves garlic, minced
1 medium yellow onion, chopped small
Two 18.3-ounce jars Jovial diced tomatoes*
½ cup fresh cilantro, chopped
½ cup fresh parsley, chopped
1 red bell pepper, diced
1 Tbsp powdered turmeric, freshly ground
1 Tbsp powdered cumin
1 tsp powdered garlic
1 tsp powdered onion
2 Tbsp extra virgin coconut oil or red palm oil
1½ tsp unrefined salt
1½ tsp black pepper

Toppings

1 cup Organic Valley* raw cheddar cheese, shredded
1 cup Kalona Super Natural* sour cream
1 cup onion, thinly sliced

Snacks

Delicious Raw Granola Bars	152
Toni's Easy and Healthy Trail Mix	155
Strawberry Oatmeal Maca Muffins	157
High-Protein Nourishing Snack	158

Chapter
Ten

Delicious Raw Granola Bars

Makes 16 bars

Ingredients

1 cup packed dates, pitted (Deglet Noor or medjool)*
¼ cup raw honey or real maple syrup
¼ cup creamy raw almond butter
1 cup raw walnuts, loosely chopped
1½ cups rolled oats
½ cup raw cacao nibs
¼ cup unsweetened, dried cranberries
1 Tbsp extra virgin coconut oil
½ cup shredded coconut (optional)
1 Tbsp vanilla extract

Directions

Using a food processor, chop the dates and cranberries for about 60 seconds, or until only small pieces remain. The dates should have a texture resembling dough. Add walnuts and shredded coconut. Set aside in separate bowl.

Mix almond butter, coconut oil, vanilla, and honey. Pour over ingredients in bowl, taking care to break up the dates so they are distributed evenly.

Line a small pan (8x8 works well) with parchment paper and add the mixture. Flatten with hands until evenly spread. Cover with parchment or plastic wrap, and place in the refrigerator or freezer to harden, about 15–20 minutes. Using the parchment paper, lift bars from pan and chop into 16 even bars. Store in an airtight container up to a few days. You may also store them in the freezer to keep them extra fresh, but it isn't necessary.

Tip

If your dates don't feel sticky and moist, soak them in water for 10 minutes and then drain before processing. This will help hold the bars together.

Health Tip

When I think raw cacao, the first word that enters my mind is antioxidants. Raw cacao is the original chocolate and is loaded with vital nutrition. Cacao is one of the world's richest sources of iron, magnesium, and selenium, some of the most valuable minerals for a healthy heart. About 70 percent of the chocolate grown around the world is laden with a variety of chemical fertilizers and is highly processed.

These chemical weapons have the potential to destroy our health over time. They deplete the soil, leaving the food less nutritious and deliver a host of poisons that lead to disease. The difference between raw cacao and cocoa is huge. Cacao is the purest and original form of chocolate and is low temperature dried, leaving all the valuable nutrients present whereas cocoa is high-heat processed. This high temperature processing damages all the enzymes, nutrients, and minerals, making this product much less nutritious and a highly allergenic food.

I believe that no one is allergic to real chocolate; they are allergic to what's been done to it. The body was uniquely designed with wisdom to detect what doesn't belong. I have witnessed clients of mine consume raw cacao treats at my events and have absolutely no allergic reaction, even though they had experienced an allergy to chocolate previously.

I highly recommend that you stick with food in the form God created to receive the abundance of natural ingredients that only nature can provide. As soon as we begin altering God's magnificent creations, problems will occur.

Toni's Easy and Healthy Trail Mix

Makes 6 servings

Directions

Mix all ingredients in a medium bowl.

This makes a highly nutritious snack to take with you on the run. Enjoy!

Ingredients

½ cup raisins
½ cup raw pumpkin seeds
½ cup dried goji berries
½ cup raw walnuts, almonds, or cashews
½ cup raw cacao nibs
½ cup unsweetened coconut flakes
1 giant scoop of love ♥

Strawberry Oatmeal Maca Muffins

Makes 12 muffins

Maca root is a Peruvian radish that has been used for centuries for balancing hormones and increasing energy. When you're craving something sweet and need an energy boost, balance your hormones by adding my Strawberry Oatmeal Maca muffins to your menu. These delicious muffins make a great snack or a quick on-the-go breakfast.

Directions

Preheat oven to 350°F.

In a large bowl, add dry ingredients, mix well, and set aside. In a medium sized bowl, beat eggs. Then, add milk, coconut oil, and vanilla. Mix. Add wet ingredients to dry ingredients and mix until creamy. Fold in strawberries.

Add baking cups to muffin tin and add about 3 tablespoons of batter to each cup. Bake for 12–15 minutes.

Enjoy hot or cooled. Store in sealed container for up to 2 weeks in refrigerator.

* Please see the Resource section for recommended brands and their availability.

Ingredients

- 1½ cups all-purpose einkorn flour*
- 1 cup coconut sugar
- 1 tsp baking soda
- ½ cup steel-cut oats, uncooked
- 3 Tbsp Sunfood.com* raw maca powder
- ½ cup fresh strawberries, quartered
- 1 Tbsp vanilla extract
- ½ tsp ground nutmeg
- 2 large eggs
- Or for egg substitute, use 2 Tbsp chia seeds
- 1 Tbsp extra virgin coconut oil, warmed
- ⅛ tsp unrefined salt
- 1 cup whole milk, coconut or dairy

Health Tip

Swap a sugar-laden soft drink for pure, infused water just by adding your favorite fruit.

Examples: apple pieces, chopped strawberries, fresh mint, and a twist of lime. Be creative!

High-Protein Nourishing Snack

Makes 1 serving

Here is my healthy, yet simple and delicious, suggestion for when you're hungry and need something quick to keep you from making a poor choice.

Directions

Peel and cut banana into bite-sized pieces and place in medium bowl. Cut, core, and remove seeds from the apple. Cut the remaining apple into bite-sized pieces, leaving the skin on or off as preferred. Add to banana and set aside.

In a small dish, add the almond butter, hemp seeds, and coconut oil. Mix well and sprinkle cinnamon on top of the fruit. Serve the almond butter mixture as a dip for your fruit.

Ingredients

1 banana
1 apple of choice
1 heaping Tbsp raw almond butter
1 Tbsp extra virgin coconut oil
1 tsp hemp seeds
⅛ tsp Ceylon cinnamon

Health Tip

Swap a prepackaged snack for a fresh piece of organic fruit dipped in organic raw nut butter of your choice.

Desserts

Toni's Delicious Banana Walnut Bread	163
Grandma Fran's Chocolate Mayonnaise Cake	165
Spicy Hot Christmas Cacao	167
Grandma Fran's Chocolate Brown Rice Pudding	169
Raw Magic Bars	171
Grandma Fran's Café Granita	173
Grandma Fran's Italian Seeded Cookies	175
Double Chocolate Chip Cookies	177
The Sweetest Sugar Cookies	179
Raw Cacao, Banana, and Avocado Mousse in Three Easy Steps	181
Easter Almond Cookies	183
Apple Crisp Delish	185
Oatmeal Cranberry Cookies	187
Interchangeable Homemade Ice Cream	189
Grandma Banfield's No-Bake Cookies	191
Michelle's Black Bean Brownies	193
Raw Rocky Road Fudge	195
Cacao Nib Chip Cookies	197
Gluten-Free Blueberry Muffins	198
Blueberry Muffins	199
RAWlicious Banana Fudge Recipe	200
Easy Raw Apricot Bars	201
Raw Cacao Fudge Truffles	202

Chapter

Eleven

The food you eat can be either the safest and most powerful form of medicine or the slowest form of poison.

– Ann Wigmore

When most people hear the word *dessert* the first thing that comes to mind is *unhealthy*. Well, let me tell you, unhealthy is farthest from the truth because it's all about the source of your ingredients. With that said, your dessert can be a very healthy food or a toxic waste.

> ### Health Tip
>
> Einkorn all-purpose flour is the alternative to modern all-purpose flour.
>
> In my first book, I wrote a chapter entitled, "Don't Go Against the Grain." In this chapter, I explain that einkorn is the original wheat. What I love about all-purpose einkorn flour is that you can bake all your favorite desserts, breads, and recipes that call for traditional all-purpose flour and your recipes will come out exactly the same. With einkorn all-purpose flour, you have all the traditional flavor without the harmful effects of modern wheat.

Toni's Delicious Banana Walnut Bread

Makes 6 servings

Directions

Preheat your oven to 350°F. Prepare a baking pan with parchment paper, or grease with coconut oil generously.

Mash the bananas and butter of choice. Using an electric hand mixer or potato masher, in a large bowl, mix until completely mashed and smooth.

Add eggs, maple syrup, honey, and vanilla to the mashed bananas and blend well. Add the baking soda, salt, cinnamon, nuts, and flour to the wet batter and blend well.

Pour the batter into the baking pan and bake for 50 minutes or until the top begins to brown and a toothpick inserted in the center of the bread comes out clean. Let the bread cool, then slice. Store covered for a few days at room temperature, in the refrigerator for a few weeks, or seal and freeze for a few months.

Top with real butter, raw almond butter, or add coconut oil and almond butter together.

Yummy! ♥

Ingredients

- 3 ripe bananas
- 3 large eggs
- ½ cup (1 stick) organic butter
- Or 5 Tbsp ghee or coconut butter
- 1 cup raw walnuts (optional)
- 6 Tbsp real maple syrup
- 1 Tbsp raw honey
- 1 Tbsp vanilla extract
- ¾ tsp baking soda
- ⅛ tsp unrefined salt
- 1 Tbsp Ceylon cinnamon
- 1 cup Bob's Red Mill* extra-fine almond flour

---

* Please see the Resource section for recommended brands and their availability.

Grandma Fran's Chocolate Mayonnaise Cake

Makes about 10 servings

With permission from my sister, Francesca Amato. She writes:

As you now know, our grandmother made a huge impact on our lives. Her legacy will live on forever through her recipes, but more importantly, in our hearts. I am proud to be named after her. When I was a little girl, I was a bit freaked out by Grandma putting mayonnaise into a chocolate cake. As it was baking, the aroma that came through the house shocked me, and I couldn't wait to have a piece or two. Don't let the mayonnaise part stop you from making this delicious recipe that is sure to please everyone's sweet tooth. My sister Toni and I used to love to lick the metal beaters.

Let's get baking!

Directions

Preheat oven to 350°F.

In a large mixing bowl, mix dry ingredients and set aside.

In another large bowl, mix the butter, mayonnaise, and vanilla with an electric hand mixer. Combine into the dry ingredients and mix on a low speed. Add in the milk slowly until all ingredients are fully combined. Grease an 8x8 baking pan with coconut oil and evenly add batter. Bake 35–40 minutes. While the cake is baking, prepare the icing by mixing the butter, vanilla, powdered sugar, and raw cacao with an electric hand mixer and set aside. Let cool completely for an hour before adding icing. When cake is fully cooled, cover the top and sides of the cake with icing and serve.

Ingredients

1 cup Chosen Foods mayonnaise*
1½ cups David Wolfe* organic sun-dried cane juice crystals
1 Tbsp pure vanilla extract
2 cups all-purpose einkorn flour*
6 Tbsp raw cacao powder
2 tsp baking powder
1 cup whole milk
4 Tbsp (½ stick) unsalted butter
⅛ tsp unrefined salt

Icing

1 cup (2 sticks) unsalted butter, softened
4 Tbsp raw cacao powder
1 cup organic powdered sugar
1 tsp pure vanilla extract

* Please see the Resource section for recommended brands and their availability.

Spicy Hot Christmas Cacao

Makes 1 serving

Directions

In a small stainless pot, add all ingredients except the cream and stir on medium to low heat. Allow mixture to come to a boil. Pour into a coffee mug. Add the cream and splash with cinnamon or raw cacao powder.

Serve hot and enjoy!

Ingredients

8 ounces filtered water
1 Tbsp raw cacao powder (not cocoa)
⅛ tsp Ceylon cinnamon
1 pinch of powdered ginger
1 Tbsp raw honey or real maple syrup
1 tsp vanilla extract
1 Tbsp coconut heavy cream

Grandma Fran's Chocolate Brown Rice Pudding

Makes 4 servings

As you now know, Grandma loved chocolate. She also enjoyed rice pudding, but she preferred to make it with the crunchy texture of brown rice.

Directions

Follow the directions on the rice package and set aside the cooked rice.

In a medium stainless pot, heat 1½ cups of milk, heavy cream, and salt on low to medium heat. Set aside the other ½ cup milk. Add the raw cacao powder and coconut sugar to the pot and mix well.

In a medium bowl, whisk together the cornstarch and the reserved ½ cup milk. Now add the cornstarch and milk mixture to the warm cacao. Mix well and bring to a boil while stirring constantly for 2 minutes after it begins to boil. Lower the heat and allow to simmer for an additional minute. Remove from heat and stir in the brown rice, vanilla, and cinnamon.

Place rice pudding in an airtight container. Sprinkle additional cinnamon on top and store in the refrigerator for up to 4 days.

Ingredients

- ½ cup uncooked brown rice (makes 1 cup cooked)
- 2 cups whole milk of choice, coconut or dairy
- ½ cup heavy cream, coconut or dairy
- ⅛ tsp unrefined salt
- 2 tsp vanilla extract
- ½ cup coconut sugar
- ½ tsp Ceylon cinnamon
- 5 Tbsp raw cacao powder
- 3 Tbsp Rapunzel* organic cornstarch

* Please see the Resource section for recommended brands and their availability.

Raw Magic Bars

Makes 16 servings

Directions

Pulse pecans in a food processor until they become crumbly, then add dates and pulse until mixed well.

Add cacao, maple syrup or honey, vanilla extract, salt, almond butter, coconut oil, coconut butter, and coconut flakes. Mix until well blended.

Press the entire mixture into an 8x8 square pan lined with parchment paper until mixture is flattened evenly. Freeze for 2 hours. Remove solid mixture from freezer and lift with parchment paper, turning the solid mixture upside down on a cutting board. Remove paper and cut into 2-inch squares with a sharp knife. Store in an airtight container in the refrigerator for up to 2 weeks.

If they last that long.

Ingredients

- 2 cups medjool dates, pitted
- 2 cups raw pecans
- ½ cup raw crunchy almond butter
- 1 Tbsp extra virgin coconut oil
- 2 Tbsp coconut butter (manna)
- 1 cup unsweetened coconut flakes
- 4 Tbsp raw cacao powder (not cocoa)
- 1 tsp vanilla extract
- 4 Tbsp raw honey or real maple syrup
- ⅛ tsp unrefined salt

Grandma Fran's Café Granita

Makes 6 servings

When I was a little girl, I loved the aroma of freshly brewed espresso, but I wasn't allowed to have it. My grandma would make this delicious Italian coffee ice and top it off with fresh whipped cream. My mom loved it and was always the one who would ask Grandma to make her homemade coffee ice, also known as "Café Granita." I was allowed to have it because it was considered a dessert.

Yay for me!

Directions

Prepare the espresso by following the directions on package, adding 2 additional tablespoons of the dried coffee grounds to make the coffee. When it becomes ice, coffee flavor weakens. By adding additional grounds, it will hold its robust flavor.

In a large bowl, stir together the hot espresso and sugar until the sugar completely dissolves. Pour the espresso mixture into a medium baking dish and transfer to the freezer. Freeze for a total of 6 hours and scrape coffee ice into serving bowls. Add cream topping and serve with a Biscotti Regina (see page 175)

Grandma always said, there's no need to add sugar to the cream since the ice has enough.

Ingredients

2 cups freshly brewed espresso

1½ cups znaturalfoods.com* evaporated cane juice crystals

Topping

1 cup heavy cream or 1 cup coconut heavy cream (works just as well)

1 Tbsp vanilla extract

* Please see the Resource section for recommended brands and their availability.

Grandma Fran's Italian Seeded Cookies

a.k.a. Biscotti Regina

Makes 5 dozen

During the holidays, I love to get creative and if I don't stop myself, I would be making every kind of cookie I could imagine. Baking and cooking is so much fun to me, not only do I love the creations, but the different aromas always bring me back to my childhood. This is one of my childhood favorites.

As a child, I used to love to bake with Grandma. The scent of vanilla extract always reminds me of her, even though she's no longer here. It's amazing how certain aromas from food bring me back to Grandma's kitchen. My sister Francesca and I always asked Grandma when she was going to make the cookies with the seeds. Our mom loved to dunk them in her coffee. She still does, even to this day.

Directions

Preheat the oven to 375ºF.

In a large bowl add eggs, coconut sugar, coconut shortening, baking powder, and anise and vanilla extracts. Mix all ingredients with an electric hand mixer. Add flour and mix well.

Take a 2-inch piece of dough and roll into ½-inch thick logs, approximately 2 inches in length. Repeat until all the dough is formed into the same shape. Place each raw cookie in milk, wetting the entire cookie. Then roll in the sesame seeds, covering the entire cookie.

Ingredients

3 cups all-purpose einkorn flour*
1 cup coconut sugar
3 large eggs
1 cup coconut shortening
2 tsp baking powder
2 tsp anise extract
1 tsp vanilla extract
1½ cups milk, your choice
2 cups raw sesame seeds

Place all the cookies on a baking sheet lined with parchment paper and bake for 20 minutes.

Remove from oven and allow to cool for about 10 minutes. Serve immediately or store in an airtight container for up to 3 weeks.

Double Chocolate Chip Cookies

Makes 3 dozen cookies

Directions

Preheat oven to 350°F.

Combine dry ingredients in one bowl. Cream butter and sugar in separate bowl and then add remaining wet ingredients. Then, mix all the ingredients together. Add chips, stirring to distribute. Line cookie sheet with parchment paper. Use 1 heaping teaspoon of batter for each cookie. Place one inch apart and bake for 10 minutes. Let cool and remove from cookie pan and serve.

* Please see the Resource section for recommended brands and their availability.

Ingredients

2 1/2 cups all-purpose einkorn flour*
1 tsp Bob's Red Mill* baking soda
1/2 tsp unrefined salt
1/2 cup (1 stick) unsalted butter, softened
12 ounces of David Wolfe's* raw chocolate chips
1/2 cup Navitas* raw cacao powder
1/2 cup coconut shortening
1 1/2 cups coconut sugar
2 tsp vanilla extract
2 large eggs

The Sweetest Sugar Cookies

Makes 3 dozen

Directions

Preheat oven to 350°F.

In a large mixing bowl, cream together butter, sugar, egg, lemon juice, and vanilla. Set aside. In another bowl, add dry ingredients and mix well. Add dry ingredients into wet ingredients and mix together to form a dough. Roll into 1-inch balls and place on cooking sheet lined with parchment paper.

Bake for 8–10 minutes or until pale beige. Let cool for 5 minutes and serve. Keep in airtight container up to two weeks.

Ingredients

2½ cups all-purpose einkorn flour*
1½ cups pure sugar cane crystals*
1 tsp baking powder
1 tsp baking soda
⅛ tsp unrefined salt
1 cup (2 sticks) unsalted butter, softened
1 Tbsp vanilla extract
1 large egg
1 Tbsp fresh lemon juice
   Or 1 tsp lemon extract

* Please see the Resource section for recommended brands and their availability.

Raw Cacao, Banana, and Avocado Mousse in Three Easy Steps

Makes 4 servings

Directions

1. In a food processor, pulse all the ingredients until blended and smooth (about 2 minutes).

2. Transfer mixture to 4 serving bowls. Chill in the fridge for 30 minutes before serving.

3. Serve and enjoy. Mousse can be stored in a refrigerator for up to 3 days.

Ingredients

2 very ripe bananas
1 ripe avocado
1 Tbsp chia seeds
2 Tbsp coconut heavy cream
4 Tbsp raw cacao powder, not cocoa
2–3 Tbsp raw honey
Or ½ cup of dates, pitted
1 Tbsp vanilla extract
1 tsp extra virgin coconut oil

Easter Almond Cookies

Makes 5 dozen cookies

It was about a week before Easter, and I was experiencing a yearning for almond cookies. So, I put on my thinking cap and came up with these. I hope you enjoy!

Directions

Preheat oven to 350°F.

In a large bowl, cream together butter and sugar. Then, mix in the egg and extracts until you reach a creamy consistency. Combine the flour, baking soda, and salt. Then add this mixture to the creamed butter and sugar. Blend well to make a dough. Roll dough into 1-inch balls. Place them 2 inches apart on a cookie sheet lined with parchment paper, leaving the cookie dough in the shape of a ball. Push one almond into center of each cookie.

Bake for 15 minutes and remove from oven. Cool for 15 minutes and serve or store in an airtight container up to 3 weeks.

Ingredients

1 cup (2 sticks) butter, softened
1 cup coconut sugar
2 eggs
1½ Tbsp almond extract
1 Tbsp vanilla extract
3 cups all-purpose einkorn flour*
1 tsp baking soda
½ tsp fine Celtic salt
About 60 raw almonds

Apple Crisp Delish

Makes 16 servings

Directions

Preheat oven to 350ºF.

After melting the coconut oil, add all filling ingredients to a medium-sized bowl, including the melted coconut oil. Mix well, covering the apples completely, and set aside.

After melting the coconut butter, add all topping ingredients, including the melted coconut butter, to a medium sized bowl. Mix well.

In a 9x13 baking pan, add additional coconut oil and evenly distribute to cover the bottom of pan. Add the filling to the pan, covering the bottom. Next, add the topping, covering the filling. Then, drizzle the 2 additional tablespoons of pure maple syrup over the top.

Bake for 40 minutes and serve as is or with any ice cream from this chapter.

Keep up to 5 days in an airtight container in refrigerator or up to 3 months in freezer.

Ingredients

For the filling:

8 apples of choice, cut into wedges, seeds and core removed (Leaving the peel on is optional.)
1 tsp fresh lemon juice
2 Tbsp extra virgin coconut oil, melted
Or 2 Tbsp ghee or butter
½ cup coconut sugar
1 Tbsp extra virgin coconut oil (for baking pan)

Topping

2 cups Go Raw* raw apple cinnamon sprouted granola
½ cup pure maple syrup
½ Tbsp Ceylon cinnamon
½ tsp fresh ginger, grated
½ tsp ground nutmeg
1 Tbsp vanilla extract
⅛ tsp unrefined salt
2 Tbsp coconut butter (manna), melted
2 Tbsp pure maple syrup (for drizzling)

* Please see the Resource section for recommended brands and their availability.

Oatmeal Cranberry Cookies

Makes 2 dozen cookies

Directions

Preheat oven to 350°F.

Mix all dry ingredients in a medium sized bowl. Cream butter and sugar, then add remaining wet ingredients and mix well. Form mixture into small 1-inch balls. Flatten with palm of hand on cookie sheet lined with parchment paper. Bake for 9–12 minutes.

Store in an airtight container for up to 3 weeks.

* Please see the Resource section for recommended brands and their availability.

Ingredients

- 1½ cups coconut sugar
- 1 cup (2 sticks) unsalted butter, softened
- 1 cup all-purpose einkorn flour*, sifted
- 1 cup rolled oats, uncooked
- 1 Tbsp extra virgin coconut oil, melted
- 2 eggs
- ½ cup dried unsweetened cranberries
- 1 Tbsp vanilla extract
- 1 Tbsp Ceylon cinnamon
- 1 tsp baking soda, sifted together with flour
- ⅛ tsp unrefined salt

Interchangeable Homemade Ice Cream

Makes 4 servings

On a hot summer day, a bowl of your favorite ice cream surely does the trick. Lickity-split!

Directions

Combine all ingredients in food processor and pulse until thick. Freeze for 2 hours and enjoy. Keeps up to 6 weeks.

Variations:

For *Chocolate Ice Cream,* follow the above recipe, then add 3–4 tablespoons raw cacao.

For *Strawberry Ice Cream,* follow the above recipe, then add 2 cups frozen strawberries.

Base Ingredients for Vanilla Ice Cream

- 2 cups raw dairy cream
    - Or coconut heavy cream (for non-dairy preference)
- 1 cup raw dairy milk
    - Or plain coconut milk (non-dairy)
- 2 frozen bananas
- 1 cup real maple syrup or raw honey
- 1 Tbsp vanilla extract

Interchangeable Homemade Ice Cream (Con't)

Added with permission from my beautiful niece, Michelle Lee Banfield. She writes:

Some of the most distinct memories that I have of my great-grandmother growing up are her love of laughter, watching dancing programs (as she called them) on TV, teaching me lessons on how to keep up with chores around the home, her daily morning leg exercises that she did well into her eighties, but most importantly her love of chocolate!

From fresh morning cocoa with cereal on a breakfast tray, to her favorite rocky road ice cream treat, the smell of chocolate still brings me back to the thought of her. And how appropriate because like my "Big Grandma" as I called her, nothing else in the world is as memorable, full of warmth with just the right amount of sweetness as this recipe for Rocky Road Ice Cream made specifically with her in mind.

For a healthier version of **Grandma Fran's Rocky Road Ice Cream,** follow the base ingredients for chocolate ice cream and fold in the following:

½ cup chopped raw walnuts
    Or nuts of choice
½ cup unsweetened, frozen coconut chunks

Note:

Do not add nuts and coconut chunks into the food processor or they will blend. Rocky road ice cream should be chunky, not smooth.

Grandma Banfield's No-Bake Cookies

Makes 5 dozen cookies

With permission from my dear niece, Michelle Banfield.

Another grandmother that I hold dear to my heart is my paternal grandma, Grandma Banfield. I remember spending summers visiting her farmhouse in the country. My grandma would play with my hair to help me sleep when I was homesick, which made me feel truly comforted and loved. She would make these easy no-bake cookies that were amazingly delicious. These cookies became an instant lifelong favorite of mine that always evoke the memory of my dear Grandma Banfield. Her cookies convey that relaxed and comforting feeling of my childhood summers at her house, just as I remember.

Although the cookies called for cocoa powder and other refined ingredients, I suggest using raw cacao powder for the maximum health benefit of raw cacao. I switched to coconut sugar and other pure organic ingredients to make them a healthier version of the original. The raw cacao powder is my added spin on her recipe, and I'm sure she would have been proud nonetheless.

Directions

In saucepan, melt butter on medium heat. Add milk, cacao powder, salt, and vanilla extract to melted butter. Mix well and simmer for about 1 minute. Next, add the peanut butter and coconut sugar. Mix well. Then, add oats and mix well. Remove from the heat and drop 1 heaping tablespoon of cookie dough onto a serving platter.

These cookies are ready to eat and enjoy.

Ingredients

- ½ cup raw cacao powder
- 2 cups coconut sugar
- ½ cup whole milk (coconut or dairy)
- 2 Tbsp melted butter (coconut or dairy)
- ⅛ tsp unrefined salt
- ½ cup crunchy jungle peanut butter
- 1 tsp pure vanilla extract
- 3 cups Bob's Red Mill* quick-cooking, steel-cut oats

Michelle's Black Bean Brownies

Make 8 brownies

I am so excited to share this next recipe with permission from my courageous, beautiful client named Michelle Aiello Ciferri.

Michelle came to me with one hundred pounds to lose, on thyroid medication, asthma medication—which included prednisone—low energy, trouble breathing, on high blood pressure medication, and was on a breathing machine. Michelle couldn't walk much, and had tremendous back, knee, and spine pain.

After exclusively following the plan I created for her specific needs, Michelle is off all her medications, feels better than she ever has, enjoys amazing energy levels, walks normally with stride, breathes well without any complications, and is totally off her breathing machine. Her blood pressure is perfect and her thyroid is completely healed, both without medication. Michelle is completely pain-free and most of all, she lost one hundred pounds.

Here is Michelle's delicious brownie recipe that she enjoys on her healthy lifestyle journey and would like to share with you.

Directions

Put all ingredients in a food processor until smooth. Bake at 350ºF for 20–25 minutes in pan lined with parchment paper. Remove from oven and let cool.

Ingredients

- 1 can of black beans, drained and rinsed
- ½ cup of raw cacao powder
- ½ cup raw honey or coconut sugar
- 3 eggs
  - Or 3 Tbsp chia seeds
- 1 tsp vanilla extract
- ½ cup of unsalted butter or coconut oil
- 1 pinch of unrefined salt

Raw Rocky Road Fudge

Makes 6–10 servings

Directions

Add all ingredients to food processor. Blend well for 1–2 minutes. Remove blended mixture carefully from processor and press contents onto wax paper in a small, square glass baking dish. Flatten down until it forms a square and freeze for 2 hours.

Remove from freezer, cut into mini squares, and enjoy.

No need to store the leftovers because there won't be any!

Ingredients

2 cups of pitted dates
1 Tbsp extra virgin coconut oil
½ cup dried coconut flakes
⅛ tsp unrefined salt
1 Tbsp vanilla extract
½ cup raw hazelnuts or any raw nut
1 Tbsp raw hemp seeds
4–6 Tbsp raw cacao powder (not cocoa)

Health Tip

Swap your negative attitude toward yourself and others for becoming a positive influence.

Cacao Nib Chip Cookies

Makes 3 dozen cookies

Directions

Preheat oven to 375ºF. Coat baking sheets with coconut oil or line with parchment paper.

Combine flour, baking soda, and salt in large bowl. Stir in almond butter, maple syrup, butter, and vanilla until blended. Fold in cacao nibs. Drop 2 tablespoons dough for each cookie onto prepared baking sheet and flatten slightly.

Bake 15–17 minutes or until golden brown. Cool 5 minutes and then transfer to wire rack to cool completely.

Add Love ♥ *and enjoy!*

Health Tip

Surprise everyone with these delicious healthy, happy, life-giving swaps.

Ingredients

½ cup crunchy almond butter
¼ cups all-purpose einkorn flour*
1 tsp baking soda
1 tsp unrefined salt
1½ cups real maple syrup
    Or 1½ cups raw honey
    Or 1½ cups coconut sugar
1 tsp vanilla extract
1½ cups organic raw cacao nibs*
1 egg
2 sticks butter, softened
1 Tbsp coconut oil (for greasing pan)

Substitutions

To substitute for the egg, choose **one** of the following:

2 Tbsp mashed avocado
1 Tbsp chia seeds and 3 Tbsp filtered water (Whisk until it becomes a jelly-like consistency and add to the recipe)

To substitute for the butter, choose **one** of the following:

½ cup melted coconut butter
½ cup melted coconut oil

* Please see the Resource section for recommended brands and their availability.

Gluten-Free Blueberry Muffins

Makes 12 servings

Directions

Preheat oven to 350°F. Grease 6–8 large muffin cups with coconut oil or butter.

Set aside 2 tablespoons of almond flour. In a mixing bowl or food processor, combine remaining 2 cups almond flour, coconut flour, and salt.

In a separate bowl, whisk together eggs, honey, and vanilla. Add this mixture to dry ingredients and blend thoroughly. Gently fold in blueberries, then pour batter into 6–8 large cups. Pat tops down into rounded heaps and use a brush to dab with melted butter. Sprinkle with remaining almond flour for a pretty finish. Bake for 30 minutes.

Ingredients

2 cups almond flour
½ cup coconut flour
6 eggs
½ cup raw honey
¾ tsp vanilla
½ tsp unrefined salt
1 cup frozen or fresh blueberries
1 Tbsp butter, melted
   Or extra virgin coconut oil

Blueberry Muffins

Makes 12 servings

Directions

Preheat oven to 375°F. With coconut oil, grease a muffin tin that holds 6 large or 12 regular-sized muffins.

In a medium-sized bowl, beat butter until creamy. Add sugar and beat until pale and fluffy. Add eggs one at a time, beating after each. Add vanilla, baking powder, and salt. Mix.

With spoon, fold in half of flour then half of milk into batter; repeat. Fold in blueberries. Spoon into muffin cups. Bake 20–25 minutes until golden brown.

Always serve with love! ♥

Ingredients

½ cup (1 stick) butter, softened
1 cup coconut sugar
2 large eggs
1 tsp vanilla extract
2 tsp baking powder
¼ tsp unrefined salt
2 cups all-purpose einkorn flour*
½ cup whole milk
1½ cups fresh or frozen blueberries

RAWlicious Banana Fudge Recipe

Makes 12 servings

Directions

Combine and process all ingredients in a food processor until smooth, roughly five minutes or so. Using a sealable container lined with parchment paper, scoop the mixture into the container, spreading evenly. Place the container in the freezer for 6 hours or overnight.

Remove from freezer and cut into squares.

For best results, keep the fudge cold by storing in the freezer so it will keep its shape. Storing in the fridge will result in a softer texture.

Next step, you'll know what to do from here. LOL!

Ingredients

- ½ cup raw coconut butter*
- 1 Tbsp hemp seeds
- 1 Tbsp raw almond or cashew butter
- 2 small ripe bananas, cut into 1-inch chunks
- ¼ cup plus 1 Tbsp cup raw cacao powder
- ½ cup raw walnuts
- 3 Tbsp raw honey or real maple syrup
- 1 tsp vanilla extract
- ¼ tsp Ceylon cinnamon

* Please see the Resource section for recommended brands and their availability.

Easy Raw Apricot Bars

Makes about 16 servings

Directions

In a food processor, slowly add apricots and dates. Mix for 1 minute. Then, add the nuts and mix for another minute. Add the salt, cinnamon, seeds, vanilla, and coconut. Mix for another minute or until all ingredients are combined.

Press the entire mixture into 8x8 square pan lined with parchment paper until mixture is flattened down and even. Freeze for 2 hours. Remove from freezer and lift solid mixture with parchment paper and turn upside down on a cutting board. Remove paper and cut into 2-inch squares with a sharp knife. Store in an airtight container in the refrigerator for up to 2 weeks.

Ingredients

1 cup raw walnuts or almonds
1 cup unsweetened coconut flakes
1 cup dried apricots
2 cups medjool dates, pitted
1 Tbsp vanilla powder
1 Tbsp hemp seeds
⅛ tsp Ceylon cinnamon
⅛ tsp unrefined salt

Raw Cacao Fudge Truffles
a.k.a. I Need Chocolate!

Makes 12–16 truffles

Here's my amazingly delicious raw cacao recipe that will assure your taste buds that these healthy desserts not only taste incredible, but benefit your health as well.

Directions

Add all your ingredients together in a food processor or high speed blender and pulse for 2–3 minutes until well combined. Remove from food processor and roll into 1-inch balls. Dust truffles in cacao powder and place in a plastic container or baking pan lined with parchment paper and freeze for 1 hour and serve.

Magical Ingredients

8 Tbsp raw cacao powder (not cocoa)
½ cup sprouted almonds
½ cup raw honey
1 Tbsp vanilla extract
1 Tbsp extra virgin coconut oil
⅛ tsp unrefined salt
1 Tbsp raw cacao powder (for dusting)

Chapter Twelve

Dining Out and Vacationing

People ask me all the time what to do when they go out to eat or are on vacation. Dining out can very well present a problem if you don't do your homework.

Here are my top six suggestions for dining out and eating on vacation:

1. Search the internet for restaurants, health food stores, and farmers' markets in the area that you plan to visit. Call and ask questions prior to dining out, such as whether or not they have any organic items on the menu. Ask if they have any local or grass-fed meat and organic or pasture-raised chicken and eggs.

2. Ask if their fish is wild or farmed raised. Now, of course you want wild caught since you've learned about the health dangers of eating farmed fish in my previous book. Ask what oils they cook with. If they use oils that are unhealthy, request that they either steam your food or cook in butter. Ask your server for a side of fresh raw onion, garlic, and lemon wedges since they all contain antimicrobial properties. Or, feel free to bring your own crushed garlic in a tiny container to eat with your meal. Most importantly, always bring with you a small container of unrefined salt. Unrefined salt is loaded with antibacterial compounds that will retard the growth of any unfriendly bacteria in your food. The minerals that are in unrefined salt also work as catalysts to aid in proper digestion.

3. Take digestive enzyme supplements to help restore the loss of enzymes in the food. Enzymes are a catalyst to help digest, break down, and metabolize your food. Although these catalysts should be naturally occurring in your food, that's not always the case when dining out.

> **Health Tip**
>
> Enzyme supplement suggestions are listed in the Resource section of this book.

4. Request a refrigerator in your hotel room so you can store your fresh, organic food that you just purchased from the health food store near your vacation spot. If a refrigerator is not available, bring a large cooler filled with all your healthy options. You can also fill your cooler with plenty of healthy options once you have reached your vacation destination. Cookies, chips, and candy bars may leave you feeling sick and ruin your getaway. I pack a blender and a juicer so I can continue my regular, healthy eating program. If it's totally impossible for you to take an electric appliance, then, by all means, take an organic, green juice powder and blender bottle. In addition, be sure to stock good quality water in your room.

5. Avoid the bread on the table since it will only cause abdominal bloating and discomfort. As you now know, that white flour cannot be digested properly due to its lack of enzymes that are catalysts helping us digest our food.

6. Load up on more greens and fresh veggies, choosing them over white rice and fries. Avoid the pasta. I promise you will feel satisfied, energetic, and ready to continue your time away. Others in your group who make poor choices may feel tired, gassy, and need a nap or an antacid.

In my opinion, there really aren't any wise choices if we don't do our homework prior to dining out. We then leave ourselves with only bad or worse choices.

You don't want to fit in and be like the rest because you were not created to fit in, you were created to stand out and make a difference. Remember, you were created in God's image; and therefore, you are a leader.

The good news is that there is a movement encouraging people to become more in tune with their health and what they put in their bodies. Therefore, healthy foods and restaurants are becoming more readily available because they are in demand. We are now seeing more juice bars, organic eateries, and locally sourced establishments that support small family farms.

Give yourself a big hand and be proud because you are a large part of the reason for this movement.

> *A man without self-control is like a city broken into and left without walls.*
>
> Proverbs 25:28, ESV

Health Tip

Swap a store-bought juice for a fresh-pressed juice from the juicer.

Chapter Thirteen

Fresh Juices and Smoothies

I refer you to the principles found in Chapter Fifteen, "Juicing and Blending," from Stop Battling Disease & Start Building Wellness.

Juices

Flu Away	207
Better Belly	207
Sweetie Pie	208
Apple Juice Cocktail	208
Glowing Skin Juice	209
Healthy Heart Juice	209
Mexican Delight	210
The Energy Enhancer	210
Tropical Sunshine	211
Orange Dream Cycle	211

Smoothies

Vanilla Protein Power Smoothie	213
Hawaiian Delight	213
Amazingly Delicious Raw Fudge Banana Split Smoothie	214
My Daily Elixir	214

Flu Away

The Ultimate Flu Shot Juice

Makes 1–2 servings

Ingredients for Juicer

½ inch fresh turmeric
½ inch fresh ginger
1 cucumber with peel
2 oranges with peel
½ lemon with peel

After juicing add:

3 drops of oregano oil (not dropper full)
⅛ tsp Ceylon cinnamon

Stir and enjoy!

Better Belly

Ease an Upset Tummy

Makes 1–2 servings

Ingredients for Juicer

3 large carrots
½ cup fresh mint
½ inch fresh ginger
4 celery stalks
1 fennel stalk
1 green apple with peel

After juicing add:

1 tsp raw apple cider vinegar

Enjoy!

Sweetie Pie

Makes 1–2 servings

> *Ingredients for Juicer*
>
> 2 apples with peel
> 3 large carrots
> 1 medium red beet
> 1 cucumber with peel
> 1 pear with skin

Apple Juice Cocktail

Makes 1–2 servings

> *Ingredients for Juicer*
>
> 4 red apples with skin
> ½ inch fresh ginger
> ½ small lemon, peeled
>
> *After juicing add:*
>
> ⅛ tsp Ceylon cinnamon
>
> *Mix well and enjoy!*

Glowing Skin Juice

Makes 1–2 servings

> *Ingredients for Juicer*
>
> 2 oranges with peel
> ½ lemon with peel
> 2 large carrots
> 1 large tomato
> 1 large cucumber with peel
> 4 stalks celery

Healthy Heart Juice
The *Beet* Goes On . . .

Makes 1–2 servings

> *Ingredients for Juicer*
>
> 2 large beets
> 1 large cucumber
> 4 romaine lettuce leaves
> 1 red apple with skin

Mexican Delight

Makes 1–2 servings

Ingredients for Juicer

1 cucumber with peel
1 lime with peel
½ cup fresh cilantro
1 red apple with peel
4 celery stalks
1 bell pepper

The Energy Enhancer

Makes 1–2 servings

Ingredients for Juicer

4 stalks celery
½ lemon with peel
1 green apple with peel
1 zucchini with peel
3 large carrots
4 kale leaves
½ cup fresh parsley
1–2 broccoli stems

Tropical Sunshine

Makes 1–2 servings

Ingredients for Juicer

1 cup fresh pineapple
1 cucumber with peel
1 cup mango
1 small lime, peeled
1 peach

After juicing:

Removed any pulp and add 6 ounces of fresh, raw coconut water.

Stir and enjoy.

Orange Dream Cycle

Makes 1–2 servings

Ingredients for Juicer

3 oranges with peel
4 celery stalks
4 large carrots
1 red apple with peel
1 medium beet
1 cucumber with peel
½ inch fresh ginger

Health Tip

Swap artificial sweeteners for real, organic raw honey.

Vanilla Protein Power Smoothie

Makes 1 serving

Ingredients

1 cup raw coconut water
⅓ cup raw coconut cream
1 tsp raw maca powder
1 cup frozen wild blueberries
1 banana
1 Tbsp raw coconut oil
1 scoop vanilla bone broth powder
1 Tbsp raw hemp seeds
1 Tbsp chia seeds
1 Tbsp raw bee pollen granules
½ tsp Ceylon cinnamon

Blend and enjoy. ♥

Hawaiian Delight

Makes 1 serving

Ingredients

4 ounces raw coconut water
½ banana
½ cup raw coconut meat
    Or 2 Tbsp raw coconut butter
4 chunks frozen mango
4 chunks frozen pineapple
4 whole strawberries
1 handful frozen blueberries
1 tsp raw honey
1 tsp raw maca powder
1 tsp organic vanilla extract
1 tsp raw coconut oil

Blend and enjoy!

Amazingly Delicious Raw Fudge Banana Split Smoothie

Makes 1 serving

Ingredients

4 ounces raw grass-fed milk
    Or 4 ounces raw coconut milk
2 Tbsp raw cacao
½ tsp Ceylon cinnamon
1 tsp vanilla extract
½ cup frozen wild blueberries
1 Tbsp bee pollen granules
1 Tbsp raw noni powder
1 Tbsp raw hemp seeds
1 ripe banana
1 tsp raw honey

Blend for 1 minute.

After blending:

Add 2 tablespoons plain whole milk yogurt and swirl on top.

Enjoy. OMG!

My Daily Elixir

Makes 1 serving

Directions

Blend for 1 minute. Pour contents into a bowl.

Add:

½ cup raw almonds
½ cup Go Raw* apple cinnamon sprouted granola

Enjoy with a spoon.

Ingredients

½ cup Harmless Harvest* raw coconut water
1 tsp vanilla extract
1 cup wild frozen blueberries
1 ripe banana
1 tsp maca powder
1 Tbsp hemp seeds
1 Tbsp extra virgin coconut oil
1 Tbsp raw bee pollen granules
1 tsp Ceylon cinnamon

Chapter Fourteen

Cooking and Baking Equipment

I am so excited that you've read all the recipes for delicious meals, desserts, and snacks in this book. Now, it's time to reflect on Chapter Twenty-one from *Stop Battling Disease & Start Building Wellness,* "What's Cooking America?" I realize that you've learned a lot about what to cook and bake in—and what not to—but let's go over some important guidelines.

I recommend avoiding nonstick cookware and baking pans due to the toxic materials they are composed of. These pans include aluminum and Teflon, which have the potential to leach into your food when heat is applied. The toxins they release lead to Alzheimer's Disease and certain types of cancers.[1] Teflon releases a toxin specifically known as *polytetrafluoroethylene* (PTFE). Wow, that's a mouthful. This chemical causes *polymer-fumes flu,* a condition with flu-like symptoms, including fever. That's not all. Long-term use of these toxic materials can cause other serious health issues.

Some glass cookware may contain lead, which is extremely dangerous to your health. Please refer to the chapter "What's Cooking, America?" in my first book to learn about the best and worst cookware.

Here are my top suggestions for safe cooking and bakeware:

1. **Ceramic-Coated cookware** is not only safe, but it's easy to clean and cooks even better than almost any other cookware.

2. **Stoneware** is great for baking, not so great for cooking on the stove. I suggest stoneware for baking cakes, cookies, and muffins because they seem to absorb flavors more evenly.

3. **Stainless steel** is wonderful for stovetop cooking—rice, quinoa, soups, omelets, stir fries, sautéing—and yes, stainless steel oven roasting pans are great too.

---

[1] Mercola, Joseph. "First Class Study to Show Direct Link Between Alzheimer's and Aluminum Toxicity." articles.mercola.com/sites/articles/archive/2014/03/22/aluminum-toxicity-alzheimers.aspx.

4. **Cast iron** is a fantastic stovetop cooking source and is a great alternative to nonstick cookware. Be careful, though, because it traps heat quickly, and you don't want to burn yourself. As an added benefit, cast iron adds a little extra iron into our diets.

   Cleaning cast iron may seem a bit tricky but let me assure you, it's the easiest thing. Do not scrub it with soap or a harsh abrasive dish sponge. First, wash your skillet with hot water and a soft dish sponge to remove stuck food—use salt and hot water with the sponge. Then, season your skillet properly after it's cleaned by adding a thin layer of coconut or red palm oil. After applying the oil, place in a preheated oven of 350ºF for about a half an hour and then store your cookware in a dry place.

Now keep in mind, heat can cause chemicals in your cooking and baking supplies to leach into your food, turning your delicious creations into unhealthy disasters.

If You Care is a company that carries nontoxic and safe baking supplies, such as parchment paper, wax paper, aluminum foil, and cooking twine. They also carry both large and small baking cups for muffins and cupcakes, as well as baking sheets and filters for tea and coffee.

Chapter Fifteen

Sample Daily Menu

Sample Menus for Meat Eaters

I believe that everyone should break their fast with at least 16–20 ounces of filtered water with a tablespoon of raw apple cider vinegar and the juice of a half lemon to allow the body to release enzymes necessary for proper digestion. This beverage should be consumed daily before your morning meal.

Monday

Breakfast: *Easy Egg Frittata* (p. 42) and *Strawberry Oatmeal Maca Muffin* (p. 157)

Lunch: *Hearty Chicken Vegetable Soup* (p. 55) and a side of *Grandma Fran's Heavenly Italian Garlic Bread* (p. 99)

Dinner: *Beef Chili* (p. 150) and a side of raw sauerkraut and fresh avocado

Tuesday

Breakfast: Fresh mixed berries of choice with *Toni's Easy and Healthy Trail Mix* (p. 155)

Lunch: *Hearty Vegetable Soup with Quinoa* (p. 57)

Dinner: *Pasta Bolognese* (p. 125) over red lentil pasta and a salad

Wednesday

Breakfast: *Grandma Fran's Odd Egg Dish* (p. 45)

Lunch: *Cream of Mushroom Crockpot Chicken* (p. 124)

Dinner: *Creamy Kamut Pasta with Chicken and Broccoli* (p. 121) and a side salad

Thursday

Breakfast: *Einkorn Blueberry Pancakes* with real butter and maple syrup (p. 43)

Lunch: *Grandma Fran's Wild Flounder Salad* (p. 77) with sprouted grain bread or over fresh arugula

Dinner: *Hearty Tri-Color Lentil Soup* (p. 49) and a side of raw sauerkraut

Friday

Breakfast: A smoothie bowl of choice

Lunch: *Wild Alaskan Sockeye Salmon Teriyaki* (p. 113) and mashed sweet potatoes with a side of raw sauerkraut

Dinner*:* *Siberian Lamb Soup* (p. 56) or *Homemade Meatballs* (p. 117) and a side of quinoa pasta with the *Italian Pomodoro sauce* (p. 129)

Saturday

Breakfast: *Tonijean's Hearty Oatmeal* (p. 35)

Lunch: *Kale and Sweet Potato Salad* (p. 82)

Dinner: *Mouth-watering Chicken Franchese* (p. 135) and a side of *Grandma Fran's String Bean Salad* (p. 78)

Sunday

Breakfast: *Cinnamon Banana Walnut Pancakes* (p. 39)

Lunch: *High-Protein Kale Salad* (p. 87)

Dinner: *Pasta Bolognese* and *Homemade Meatballs* (p. 125 & 117)

The above foods should always be organic. Oils should always be organic, extra virgin, and unrefined. Coconut oil is best for cooking. Olive oil and flaxseed oil are best for drizzling on salads.

Salt should be unrefined.

Vinegar should be raw and organic.

Beef should be grass fed, eggs and chicken should be pasture-raised or organic.

All dairy should be as follows:

- Butter should be raw or organic
- Yogurt should be full-fat, organic or raw, and plain
- Milk should be certified raw and grass fed
- Kefir should be full-fat, raw or organic, and plain.

Fish should always be wild, with scales and fins, and never farmed raised.

Raw sauerkraut should be consumed with every cooked meal for optimal digestion. Raw sauerkraut contains naturally occurring live enzymes and probiotics that support gut health.

For optimal health results, I suggest a fresh raw juice be consumed daily either in between meals or before your morning meal. These recipes can be found in Chapter Thirteen.

Juice should always be freshly made from raw from organic produce, never use stored juices.

Raw nuts and seeds and fresh fruit should be eaten for snacks as a healthy alternative to processed candy bars and bagged chips.

Hunger is the first element of self-discipline. If you can control what you eat and drink, you can control everything else.
    – Dr. Umar Faruq Abd-Allah

Sample Menus for Vegetarians

Monday

Breakfast: Pick a juice recipe from Chapter Thirteen and enjoy Tonijean's Hearty Oatmeal about 20 minutes later (p. 35)

Lunch: Choose a smoothie of choice from Chapter Thirteen

Dinner: *Hearty Tri-Color Lentil Soup* (p. 49) and *Mediterranean Arugula Salad with Heirloom Tomatoes* (p. 86)

Tuesday

Breakfast: Pick a juice recipe from Chapter Thirteen and enjoy a smoothie of choice from Chapter Thirteen about 20 minutes later

Lunch: *Mango and Watermelon Salad* (p. 67)

Dinner: *Creamy Butternut Squash Soup* (p. 51) and *Red Cabbage Salad* (p. 75)

Wednesday

Breakfast: Pick a juice recipe from Chapter Thirteen and enjoy Tri-Color Quinoa Breakfast Porridge (p. 37) about 20 minutes later

Lunch: *Potato Salad: Three Ways* (p. 61)

Dinner: *Popeye's Spinach Salad* (p. 71)

Thursday

Breakfast: Pick a juice recipe from Chapter Thirteen and enjoy Cinnamon Banana Walnut Pancakes (p. 39) about 20 minutes later

Lunch: *Healing Mineral Soup* (p. 58)

Dinner: *Kale and Sweet Potato Salad* (p. 82)

Friday

Breakfast: Pick a juice recipe from Chapter Thirteen and enjoy Gluten-Free Blueberry Muffins (p. 41) about 20 minutes later

Lunch: *Delicious, Creamy Sweet Potato Soup* (p. 53)

Dinner: *What's in the Fridge Salad* (p. 83)

Saturday

Breakfast: Pick a juice recipe from Chapter Thirteen and enjoy Fluffy Coconut Pancakes (p. 44) about 20 minutes later

Lunch: *Arugula and Pear Salad with Feta* (p. 85)

Dinner: *Hearty Vegetable Soup with Quinoa* (p. 57)

Sunday

Breakfast: Pick a juice recipe from Chapter Thirteen and enjoy Strawberry Oatmeal Maca Muffins (p. 157) about 20 minutes later

Lunch: *Collard Green Spring Rolls* (p. 101)

Dinner: *Vegetarian Thai Cuisine in Seven Easy Steps* (p. 144)

Dessert options for both vegetarians and meat eaters may be found in Chapter Eleven of this book.

Eating well is a form of self-respect.
– Author unknown

What I Eat in a Day

Upon rising, I always consume a 16-ounce glass of filtered water with the juice of half of a lemon and 1 tablespoon raw apple cider vinegar. Most people can barely open their eyes until they chug down a cup of java. I feel the same way about my morning juice. I have a 20-ounce freshly made, raw juice. I alternate between the juice recipes in my first book and the recipes in this book. The vibrancy and energy that I experience each day after a fresh, raw juice goes way beyond a cup of joe.

Now if you're a coffee person, that's ok. I refer you to Chapter Seventeen of *Stop Battling Disease & Start Building Wellness*, "Coffee and Tea," where you will learn that both are healthy beverages. What makes them unhealthy is their source. In that chapter, you will learn all the reasons these beverages in their conventional form are harmful to your health. You will also learn how healthy coffee and tea can be when you choose organic. Typically, the average person drinks up to four cups of coffee daily. Chapter Seventeen explains why the overconsumption of this beverage in any form may be harmful to your health. My suggestions for coffees and teas can be found in the resource section in my first book.

I also fuel my body with whole food supplements throughout the day in the form of powders, tinctures, and capsules. You can learn all about supplements in the chapter of my first book titled, "The Truth about Supplements." My top suggestions for supplement sources are in the resource section of that first volume.

Partial fasting is a healing modality in which one will refrain from eating for 3–4 hours, or from your last meal in the evening until noon the following day. This modality allows your organs to rest so the body can repair itself. I choose to implement this practice every day after my morning water and juice cocktail. The energy and stamina that intermittent fasting gives my body is extraordinary.

My first solid meal is a smoothie bowl which is normally around 12:30 or 1:00 in the afternoon. Recipes for smoothies are included in Chapter Thirteen.

Dinner is normally a vegetarian meal, which also can be found in this book, mostly in the salad chapter. Being a vegetarian, I enjoy an abundance of fresh organic produce as well as other plant-based foods, which include healthy fats. I eat mostly raw foods, but also enjoy some of my food cooked.

I graze on fresh fruit periodically throughout the day and enjoy a raw dessert. Recipes for raw desserts are included in Chapter Eleven.

I also drink plenty of filtered water to keep my body hydrated all year round.

> *To eat is a necessity, but to eat intelligently is an art.*
> – François de La Rochefoucauld

Your future health relies on the choices you make today.

> **Health Tip**
>
> Swap an argument for a hug.

Simple Strategies for Better Health

You must make the change to be the change.

1. **Plan ahead.** Start by making a list of foods you need so you're not wandering around the store looking for unhealthy options. This way you'll have all your healthy items on hand for the recipes.

2. **Go the distance.** Stop making excuses and make time to be in the kitchen. Many people tell me that they don't have time to prepare their meals, yet they find the time to go to a movie or hit the local ice cream stand for a chemical-laden treat.

3. **Be proactive.** When you're preparing meals, make extra—also known as *bulk cooking*—so you have enough for days or even weeks ahead. Remember, you can always freeze your meals so you have them after a long work day. This strategy beats worrying about what's for dinner.

4. **Involve the family.** Get the kids and even your spouse into the kitchen, as this is a great way to implement healthy strategies for your entire family. This positive action will be appreciated by your children later in life. There's nothing like teaching our children the value of home cooking. What better time than now? In addition, more hands in the kitchen create quicker meals and satisfied, happy bellies.

5. **Last, but not least, plan a recipe night.** Have a recipe night where everyone votes on a recipe. Use your slow cooker on that day so when everyone gets home your chosen meal is waiting.

> **Health Tips**
>
> 1. Use a collard green as a substitute for bread, add your choice of healthy organic foods, roll and enjoy!
>
> 2. Carry filtered water infused with sliced fresh fruit and veggies instead of stored juices and soft drinks that pack on the pounds and create inflammation.
>
> 3. Bring raw, organic mixed nuts and organic fresh fruit as a snack instead of a chemical-laden, prepackaged snack. Raw nuts contain healthy fats that sustain your hunger by keeping your blood sugar stable.
>
> 4. Keep your thoughts and words positive. We attract what we portray.
>
> 5. Forgiveness is extremely important for our well-being. Holding grudges breeds deadly emotions. It's like drinking poison and expecting the other person to die.

Dear friend, I pray that you may enjoy good health and that all may go well with you, even as your soul is getting along well.

3 John 1:2, NIV

Conclusion

I want to thank you for reading my cookbook. I hope these recipes bring joy, happiness, and great health to you and your loved ones. Now you know that eating healthy is not about deprivation or restriction; it's about abundance and abundant health. May these recipes bring you and your family and friends together and bless you all with extraordinary health.

> *There you and your families will feast in the presence of the LORD your God, and you will rejoice in all you have accomplished because the LORD your God has blessed you.*
>
> Deuteronomy 12:7 NLT

Prayer Before Meals

Dear Heavenly Father, thank you for bringing my family and friends to the table on this day. I ask you, Lord, to bless each and everyone here with abundance of health, happiness, joy, and peace. May this meal bring each of us pleasure to our mouths and health upon our bodies. In the name of Jesus, Amen.

Bon appétit!

> *And when he had said these things, he took bread, and giving thanks to God, in the presence of all he broke it.*
>
> Acts 27:35, ESV

Resources

General Websites

beyondorganic.com
eatwild.com
realmilk.com
westonaprice.org

Cereals

emmysorganics.com
erewhonorganic.com
foodforlife.com
goraw.com (apple cinnamon raw granola)
knowfoods.com
lydiasfoods.com
onedegreeorganics.com

Chickpea breadcrumbs

watuseefoods.com

Chocolate chips, raw

longevitywarehouse.com (David Wolfe's chocolate chips)

Coconut chips, flakes, and frozen coconut chunks

dangfoods.com
eatwildrice.ca
freshdirect.com
traderjoes.com

Coconut milk and coconut cream

edwardandsons.com (Native Forest)

Coconut shortening

nutiva.com

Coconut water and kombucha

earthcircleorganics.com

Coconut butter a.k.a. manna

artisanaorganics.com
store.nutiva.com

Condiments: salt, spices, extracts

bragg.com
chosenfoods.com (mayonnaise)
frontiercoop.com
himalania.com (pink sea salt)
longevitywarehouse.com
realsalt.com
selenanaturally.com
simplyorganic.com
sunorganicfarm.com

Cornstarch

veganessentials.com

Dairy

ancientorganics.com
beyondorganic.com
butterworksfarm.com
cloversonoma.com
hawthornevalleyfarm.org
kalonasupernatural.com

kerrygold.com
maplebrookvt.com (ricotta, mozzarella and feta)
organicvalley.coop (raw cheese, ghee, butter)
pureindianfoods.com (ghee)
purityfarms.ca
sevenstarsfarm.com
stellacheese.com (mozzarella and grated cheese)
threegirlsvegan.com
traderspointcreamery.com
wallabyyogurt.com

Dates and dried fruit

madeinnature.com
nuts.com
sunfood.com

Eggs

eatwild.com
happyeggco.com
healthytraditions.com
vitalfarms.com

Flax/Hemp seed oils

barleens.com
edenfoods.com (toasted sesame oil)
longevitywarehouse.com
newmansown.com
nutiva.com
omeganutrition.com

Flours

arrowheadmills.com
coconutsecret.com
honeyville.com
jovialfoods.com (all-purpose einkorn flour)
nowfoods.com
sunfood.com

Frozen fruit, vegetables, and coconut meat

cascadianfarm.com
earthboundfarm.com
woodstock-foods.com

Grains: flours, beans, and breads

alvaradostreetbakery.com
berlinnaturalbakery.com
bobsredmill.com
edenfoods.com
foodforlife.com
healthytraditions.com
jovialfoods.com
jyotifoods.com
knowfoods.com
mannaorganicbakery.com
nuts.com
shewolfbakery.com (breads and baguettes)
sunorganicfarm.com
truroots.com

Hummus

hopefoods.com
majesticgarlic.com

Meats/Cold cuts (grass fed)

applegate.com
beyondorganic.com
eatwild.com
nutiva.com
organicprairie.com
westonaprice.org

Nut butters

artisanaorganics.com
nuts.com
rejuventative.com
store.nutiva.com
therawfoodworld.com
vivapura.com (wild raw jungle peanut butter)

Oils: cooking and cold dish

bragg.com
drbronners.com
gardenoflife.com
healthytraditions.com
nutiva.com
oliveoillovers.com
oliviersandco.com
papavince.com

Pasta

exploreasian.com
foodforlife.com
glutenfreefelicia.com (my top suggestion)
jovialfoods.com
kingsoba.com
knowfoods.com
natureslegacyforlife.com
shop.ancientharvest.com (gluten free elbow pasta)
tolerantfoods.com
truroots.com

Raw juice powders

gardenoflife.com
longevitywarehouse.com
markusrothkranz.com
organifi.com
therawfoodworld.com

Rice/quinoa

eatwildrice.ca
edenfoods.com
lundberg.com (USDA organic and sprouted only)
thrivemarket.com
truroots.com

Sauces and teriyaki

coconutsecret.com (coconut teriyaki, coconut aminos)
southrivermiso.com (garlic red pepper, soy-free miso)

Sauerkraut

bubbies.com
edenfoods.com
hawthornevalleyfarm.org
rawsuperkrauts.com
sonomabrinery.com

Snacks

buddhabowl.com (popcorn)
gnosischocolate.com
goraw.com
gowaybetter.com (chips)
hailmerry.com
heavenlyorganics.com
honeymamas.com (the best raw chocolate bars)
jacksonshonest.com (potato chips)
latejuly.com (chips)
live-live.com
madeinnature.com (dried fruit)

marysgonecrackers.com (crackers)
organicnectars.com
sejoyia.com
uniquesplits.com (sprouted pretzels)
gtslivingfoods.com
harmlessharvest.com

Sprouted nuts and trail mixes

livingintentions.com
organiclivingsuperfoods.com
sunfood.com
therawfoodworld.com

Super foods and herbs

ancientnutrition.com (vanilla bone broth protein)
dragonherbs.com
herb-pharm.com
himalania.com
hostdefense.com
jingherbs.com
livingearthherbs.com
longevitywarehouse.com
markusrothkranz.com
mountainroseherbs.com
navitasorganics.com
naturesanswer.com
pureplanet.com
realnoni.com (Hawaiian organic noni)
sunfood.com
sunwarrior.com (classic organic plus vanilla)
therawfoodworld.com
traderjoes.com
ysorganic.com
znaturalfoods.com

Sweeteners: coconut nectar, sugar, stevia, raw honey, maple syrup

bigtreefarms.com
hiddenspringsmaple.com
kenyonbee.com
longevitywarehouse.com (David Wolfe's Noniland gold honey)
madhavasweeteners.com
maplevalleysyrup.coop
nowfoods.com
nunaturals.com
quarryhillfarmmaple.com
reallyrawhoney.com
sweetleaf.com (pure green leaf stevia)
znaturalfoods.com (cane juice crystals)

Tea/coffee

7springsfarm.com
deansbeans.com
fairtradecoffee.org
jimsorganiccoffee.com
longevitywarehouse.com
mightyleaf.com
newmansown.com
numitea.com
organiccoffeecompany.com
organicindia.com
republicoftea.com (USDA organic only)
tazo.com (USDA organic only)
thebeancompany.com
tradtionalmedicinals.com
tulsiteaindia.com
yogitea.com

Tomato sauces

bionaturae.com
edenfoods.com
jovialfoods.com
muirglen.com

Tuna, salmon, and sardines

crownprince.com
mycadia.com
wildplanetfoods.com

Veggie burgers

hilaryseatwell.com
sunshineburger.com

Vinegar/seasonings

bragg.com
coconutsecret.com
edenfoods.com (rice vinegar)

Yogurt

browncowfarm.com
kalonasupernatural.com
maplebrookfarm.com
maplehill.com
redwoodhill.com
stonyfield.com

Index

A

Amazingly Delicious and Creamy Red Lentil Pasta Pesto, *138*, 139
Amazingly Delicious Raw Fudge Banana Split Smoothie, 214
antioxidant recipes
    High-Antioxidant Red Lentil Pasta, 148
    High-Antioxidant Salad Dressing, 92
appetite, stimulated by additives, 25
appetizers
    Avocado Dip, 107
    Cauliflower Pizza, *102*, 103
    Collard Green Spring Rolls, *100*, 101
    Grandma Fran's Bruschetta, *94*, 95
    Grandma Fran's Pesto, *96*, 97
    Grandma Fran's Heavenly Italian Garlic Bread, *98*, 99, 218
    Grandma Fran's Stuffed Mushrooms, *104*, 105
    Honey Lemon Asparagus with Slivered Almonds, *106*, 107
    Hummus, 109
    My Family's Thanksgiving Stuffing, 110
anticancer recipe, *64*, 65
anti-inflammatory recipe, *64*, 65
apple cider vinegar, 31, 217, 220
    Hearty Chicken Vegetable Soup, *54*, 55
    Potato Salad: Three Ways, *60*, 61, 219
    Sweetest Potato Salad, *72*, 73
Apple Juice Cocktail, 208
apple recipes
    Apple Crisp Delish, *184*, 185
    Apple Juice Cocktail, 208
    Better Belly (juice), 207
    Creamy Butternut Squash Soup, *50*, 51, 220
    Delicious Creamy Sweet Potato Soup, 53, 220
    Energy Enhancer, The (juice), 210
    Healthy Heart Juice, 209
    High-Protein Nourishing Snack, 158
    Kale and Sweet Potato Salad, *82*, 218, 219
    Orange Dream Cycle (juice), 211
    Red Cabbage Salad, *74*, 75, 220
    Sweetie Pie (juice), 208
    Zucchini Noodles with Creamy Walnut Pesto, 149
Apricot Bars, Easy Raw, 201
Arame Salad, *80*, 81
arugula recipes
    Arugula and Pear Salad with Feta, *84*, 85, 220
    High-Enzymatic Salad, 89
    Mediterranean Arugula Salad with Heirloom Tomatoes, 86, 219
asparagus recipes
    High-Antioxidant Red Lentil Pasta, 148
    Honey Lemon Asparagus with Slivered Almonds, *106*, 107
    Popeye's Spinach Salad, *70*, 71, 219
attitude, health tips about, 221
avocado recipes
    Avocado Dip, 107
    Collard Green Spring Rolls, *100*, 101
    High-Energy Healing Salad, *64*, 65

Raw Cacao, Banana, Avocado Mousse in Three Easy Steps, *180*, 181

B

baking equipment, 215–216

banana recipes
    Amazingly Delicious Raw Fudge Banana Split Smoothie, 214
    Cinnamon Banana Walnut Pancakes, *38*, 39, 218, 219
    Einkorn Blueberry Pancakes, 43
    Hawaiian Delight, 213
    High-Protein Nourishing Snack, 158
    Interchangeable Homemade Ice Cream, 189–90
    My Daily Elixir, 214
    Raw Cacao, Banana, Avocado Mousse in Three Easy Steps, *180*, 181
    Toni's Delicious Banana Walnut Bread, *162*, 163
    Vanilla Protein Power Smoothie, *212*, 213

beef recipes
    Beef Chili, 150, 217
    Homemade Meatballs, *116*, 117, 218
    Pasta Bolognese, 125, 217, 218

Beet Salad, *68*, 69

berries
    Einkorn Blueberry Pancakes, 43, 217
    Muffins, Gluten-Free Blueberry, *40*, 41, 198, 219

Better Belly (juice), 207

black beans
    Beet Salad, *68*, 69
    Michelle's Black Bean Brownies, *192*, 193
    Vegetarian Chili, *140*, 141

Blueberry Muffins, 199

Blueberry Muffins, Gluten-Free, *40*, 41, 198, 219

Blueberry Pancakes, Einkorn, 43, 217

bread
    Heavenly Italian Garlic Bread, Grandma Fran's, *98*, 99, 217
    Toni's Delicious Banana Walnut Bread, *162*, 163

breakfast
    "breaking your fast," 31–32
    Cinnamon Banana Walnut Pancakes, *38*, 39, 219
    Easy Egg Frittata, 42, 217
    Einkorn Blueberry Pancakes, 43, 217
    Fluffy Coconut Pancakes, 44, 219
    Gluten-Free Blueberry Muffins, *40*, 41, 198, 219
    Grandma Fran's Odd Egg Dish, 45
    Tonijean's Hearty Oatmeal, *34*, 35, 219
    Tri-Color Quinoa Breakfast Porridge, *36*, 37

broccoli
    Creamy Kamut Pasta with Chicken and Broccoli, *120*, 121, 217
    Easy Egg Frittata, 42, 217
    Hearty Vegetable Soup with Quinoa, 57, 217
    Red Lentil Pasta Alfredo with Broccoli, *132*, 133

Brownies, Michelle's Black Bean, *192*, 193

Bruschetta, Grandma Fran's, *94*, 95

budget for organic food, 25–27

butternut squash
    Creamy Butternut Squash Soup, *50*, 51, 220
    Hearty Chicken Vegetable Soup, *54*, 55

C

cabbage
- Arame Salad, *80*, 81
- Healing Mineral Soup, 58, 219
- Red Cabbage Salad, *74*, 75, 220
- What's in the Fridge Salad, 83, 219

cacao
- Cacao Nib Chip Cookies, *196*, 197
- raw cacao health tip, 153
- Raw Cacao, Banana, Avocado Mousse in Three Easy Steps, *180*, 181
- Raw Cacao Fudge Truffles, 202
- RAWlicious Banana Fudge Recipe, 200
- Spicy Hot Christmas Cacao, *166*, 167

Café Granita, Grandma Fran's, *172*, 173

Cake, Grandma Fran's Chocolate Mayonnaise, *164*, 165

carrots
- Collard Green Spring Rolls, *100*, 101
- Healing Mineral Soup, 58, 219
- Hearty Chicken Vegetable Soup, *54*, 55
- Hearty Tri-Color Lentil Soup, *48*, 49, 217, 219
- Hearty Vegetable Soup with Quinoa, 57, 217
- Siberian Lamb Soup, 56, 218

cauliflower
- Cauliflower Fried Rice, *130*, 131
- Cauliflower Pizza, *102*, 103

celery
- Healing Mineral Soup, 58, 219
- Hearty Chicken Vegetable Soup, *54*, 55, 218
- Hearty Tri-Color Lentil Soup, *48*, 49, 217, 219
- Hearty Vegetable Soup with Quinoa, 57, 217
- My Family's Thanksgiving Stuffing, 110
- Siberian Lamb Soup, 56, 218

cheeses in recipes, *See also* cream cheese in recipes
- Amazingly Delicious and Creamy Red Lentil Pasta Pesto, *138*, 139
- Arugula and Pear Salad with Feta, *84*, 85, 220
- Cauliflower Pizza, *102*, 103
- Creamy Kamut Pasta with Chicken and Broccoli, 121, 217
- Easy Egg Frittata, 42, 217
- Grandma Fran's Pesto, *96*, 97
- Grandma Fran's Heavenly Italian Garlic Bread, *98*, 99
- Grandma Fran's *Pasta e Piselli*, *126*, 127
- Grandma Fran's Sicilian Baked Macaroni, *118*, 119–120
- Grandma Fran's Stuffed Mushrooms, *104*, 105
- High-Protein Kale Salad, 87, 218
- Homemade Meatballs, *116*, 117, 218
- My Family's Thanksgiving Stuffing, 110
- Pasta Che Non Basta, *142*, 143
- Red Lentil Pasta Alfredo with Broccoli, *132*, 133
- Romano cheese, 146
- Vegetarian Chili, *140*, 141
- Zucchini Noodles with Creamy Walnut Pesto, 149

cherry tomatoes. *See also* tomatoes
- Arugula and Pear Salad with Feta, *84*, 85, 220
- High-Energy Healing Salad, *64*, 65

High-Enzymatic Salad, 89
High-Protein Pasta Salad, 87, 218
Popeye's Spinach Salad, *70*, 71, 219
Red Cabbage Salad, *74*, *75*, 220
What's in the Fridge Salad, 83, 219
Zucchini Pasta Italiano, *136*, 137

chicken recipes
- Cream of Mushroom Crock Pot Chicken, 124
- Creamy Kamut Pasta with Chicken and Broccoli, 121, 217
- Delicious Chicken Chili, *122*, 123
- Hearty Chicken Vegetable Soup, *54*, *55*, 218
- Mouth-Watering Chicken Franchese, *134*, 135, 219

chickpeas
- Delicious Chicken Chili, *122*, 123
- High-Energy Healing Salad, *64*, 65
- Quinoa Salad with Chickpeas, *62*, 63

chili recipes
- Beef Chili, 150, 218
- Delicious Chicken Chili, *122*, 123
- Vegetarian Chili, *140*, 141

Chocolate Brown Rice Pudding, Grandma Fran's, *168*, 169
Chocolate Mayonnaise Cake, Grandma Fran's, *164*, 165
Cinnamon Banana Walnut Pancakes, *38*, *39*, 219
coffee, 221, 228
collard green, health tip about, 221
Collard Green Spring Rolls, *100*, 101
community supported agriculture (CSA), 26
cook at home, for budget reasons, 26
cookies
- Cacao Nib Chip Cookies, *196*, 197
- Double Chocolate Chip Cookies, *176*, 177
- Easter Almond Cookies, *182*, 183
- Grandma Banfield's No-Bake Cookies, 191
- Italian Seeded Cookies, Grandma Fran's, *174*, 175
- Oatmeal Cranberry Cookies, *186*, 187
- The Sweetest Sugar Cookies, *178*, 179

cooking equipment, 215–216
coupons and discounts, 26–27
cream cheese in recipes
- Grandma Fran's Stuffed Mushrooms, *104*, 105
- Creamy Butternut Squash Soup, *50*, 51, 220
- Creamy Kamut Pasta with Chicken and Broccoli, *120*, 121, 217
- Creamy Ranch Dressing, *90*, 91

D

dairy
- guidelines for, 218
- from local sources, 26

Delicious Chicken Chili, *122*, 123
Delicious Creamy Sweet Potato Soup, 53, 220
Delicious Raw Granola Bars, 152
desserts
- Apple Crisp Delish, *184*, 185
- Apricot Bars, Easy Raw, 201
- Blueberry Muffins, 199
- Cacao Nib Chip Cookies, *196*, 197
- Double Chocolate Chip Cookies, *176*, 177
- Easter Almond Cookies, *182*, 183

Gluten-Free Blueberry Muffins, *40*, 41, 198, 219
Grandma Banfield's No-Bake Cookies, 191
Grandma Fran's Café Granita, *172*, 173
Grandma Fran's Chocolate Brown Rice Pudding, *168*, 169
Grandma Fran's Chocolate Mayonnaise Cake, *164*, 165
Grandma Fran's Italian Seeded Cookies, *175*, 17
Ice Cream, Homemade Interchangeable, *188*, 189–190
Michelle's Black Bean Brownies, *192*, 193
Muffins, Gluten-Free Blueberry, 198, 219
Oatmeal Cranberry Cookies, *186*, 187
Raw Cacao, Banana, Avocado Mousse in Three Easy Steps, *180*, 181
Raw Cacao Fudge Truffles, 202
Raw Magic Bars, *170*, 171
Raw Rocky Road Fudge, *194*, 195
Rocky Road Ice Cream, Grandma Fran's, 191
Spicy Hot Christmas Cacao, *166*, 167
Sweetest Sugar Cookies, The, *178*, 179
Toni's Delicious Banana Walnut Bread, *162*, 163
digestive enzyme supplements, for dining out, 203
dining out, six suggestions for, 203–205
dinner recipes
Amazingly Delicious and Creamy Red Lentil Pasta Pesto, *138*, 139
Beef Chili, 150, 218
Cauliflower Fried Rice, *130*, 131
Cream of Mushroom Crock Pot Chicken, 124
Creamy Kamut Pasta with Chicken and Broccoli, *120*, 121, 217
Delicious Chicken Chili, *122*, 123
Grandma Fran's Italian Style Zucchini, 146
Grandma Fran's Pasta e Piselli, *126*, 127
Grandma Fran's Sicilian Baked Macaroni, *118*, 119–120
High-Antioxidant Red Lentil Pasta, 148
Homemade Meatballs, *116*, 117, 218
Italian Pomodoro with Pasta, *128*, 129, 218
Mouth-Watering Chicken Franchese, *134*, 135, 219
Pasta Che Non Basta, *142*, 143
Pasta Bolognese, 125, 217, 218
Raw Vegan Fettuccine Alfredo, *114*, 115
Red Lentil Pasta Alfredo with Broccoli, *132*, 133
Tri-Color Quinoa Pilaf, 147
Vegetarian Chili, *140*, 141
Vegetarian Thai Cuisine in Seven Easy Steps, 144–145, 220
Wild Alaskan Sockeye Salmon Teriyaki, *112*, 113, 218
Zucchini Noodles with Creamy Walnut Pesto, 149
Zucchini Pasta Italiano, *136*, 137
Double Chocolate Chip Cookies, *176*, 177
Dressing, Creamy Ranch, *90*, 91

E

Easter Almond Cookies, *182*, 183
Easy Egg Frittata, 42, 217
eggplant
Grandma Fran's Sicilian Baked Macaroni, *118*, 119–120

Vegetarian Thai Cuisine in Seven Easy Steps, 144–145, 219
eggs
    Easy Egg Frittata, 42, 217
    Fluffy Coconut Pancakes, 44, 219
    Grandma Fran's Odd Egg Dish, 45
einkorn flour
    Blueberry Muffins, 199
    Cacao Nib Chip Cookies, *196*, 197
    Double Chocolate Chip Cookies, *176*, 177
    Eastern Almond Cookies, *182*, 183
    Einkorn Blueberry Pancakes, 43, 217
    Grandma Fran's Italian Seeded Cookies, *174*, 175
    health tip, 161
    Oatmeal Cranberry Cookies, *186*, 187
    Strawberry Oatmeal Maca Muffins, *156*, 157, 217
    Sweetest Sugar Cookies, The, *178*, 179
Energy Enhancer, The, 210
enzymes, natural stimulation of, 31

F
families, and cooking together, 221
farmers' markets, 26, 203
fasting, intermittent, 31, 220
fennel
    Better Belly (juice), 207
    Healing Mineral Soup, 58, 219
Fettuccine Alfredo, Raw Vegan, *114*, 115
fiber, versus protein, 16
fish
    guidelines for, 218
    tip for dining out, 203
    Wild Alaskan Sockeye Salmon Teriyaki, *112*, 113, 218
    Wild Flounder Salad, Grandma Fran's, 78, 218
Flu Away (juice), 207
forgiveness, health tip about, 221
Frittata, Easy Egg, 42, 217
fruit recipes. *See also* apple recipes; banana recipes; juices; smoothies
    Arugula and Pear Salad with Feta, *84*, 85, 220
    health tips, 35, 157
    Mango and Watermelon Salad, *66*, 67, 219
    natural sugars in, 16–17
    as snacks, 218
    Tropical Sunshine (juice), 211
fudge truffles, 202

G
garbanzo beans
    High-Enzymatic Salad, 89
    High-Protein Kale Salad, 87, 218
    Hummus, 109
    Kale and Sweet Potato Salad, 82
    Popeye's Spinach Salad, *70*, 71, 219
    Quinoa Salad with Chickpeas, *62*, 63
gardening, 27
garlic bread, *98*, 99, 217
genetically modified organisms (GMOs), 23
Glowing Skin Juice, *209*
gluten-free recipes
    Gluten-Free Blueberry Muffins, 198, 219
    Grandma Fran's Sicilian Baked Macaroni, *118*, 119–120
    Pasta Che Non Basta, *142*, 143

glysophate, in soil, 23
Grandma Fran's Pesto, *96*, 97
Grandma Fran's recipes
    Bruschetta, *94*, 95
    Café Granita, *172*, 173
    Chocolate Brown Rice Pudding, *168*, 169
    Chocolate Mayonnaise Cake, *164*, 165
    Heavenly Italian Garlic Bread, *98*, 99, 217
    Italian Seeded Cookies, *174*, 175
    Italian Style Zucchini, 146
    Odd Egg Dish, 45, 218
    Pasta e Piselli, *126*, 127
    Rocky Road Ice Cream, 191
    Sicilian Baked Macaroni, *118*, 119–120
    String Bean Salad, 79, 219
    Stuffed Mushrooms, *104*, 105
    Wild Flounder Salad, 78, 218
Granola Bars, Delicious Raw, 152

H
Hawaiian Delight (smoothie), 213
Healing Mineral Soup, 58
health
    smiling and, 24
    strategies for, 221
Healthy Heart Juice, 209
Hearty Chicken Vegetable Soup, *54*, 55, 218
Hearty Vegetable Soup with Quinoa, 57, 217
Hearty Tri-Color Lentil Soup, *48*, 49, 217, 219
Heavenly Italian Garlic Bread, Grandma Fran's, *98*, 99, 217
Heaven on Earth Healing Center, Inc., 21
High-Antioxidant Salad Dressing, 92
High-Energy Healing Salad, *64*, 65
High-Enzymatic Salad, 89
High-Protein Kale Salad, 87, 218
High-Protein Nourishing Snack, 158
High-Protein Pasta Salad, 88
Honey Lemon Asparagus with Slivered Almonds, *106*, 107
honey, raw, health tip about, *212*
Hummus, 109

I
Ice Cream, Homemade Interchangeable, *188*, 189–190
Italian recipes
    Grandma Fran's Café Granita, *172*, 173
    Grandma Fran's Heavenly Italian Garlic Bread, *98*, 99, 217
    Grandma Fran's Italian Seeded Cookies, *174*, 175
    Grandma Fran's Sicilian Baked Macaroni, *118*, 119–120
    Italian Pomodoro with Pasta, *128*, 129, 218
    Italian Seeded Cookies, Grandma Fran's, *174*, 175
    Italian Style Zucchini, Grandma Fran's, 146
    Pasta Che Non Basta, *142*, 143
    Pasta Bolognese, 125, 217, 218
    Pasta e Piselli, Grandma Fran's, *126*, 127
    Raw Vegan Fettuccine Alfredo, *114*, 115
    Romano cheese, 146
    Zucchini Pasta Italiano, *136*, 137

J
juices. *See also* smoothies
    Apple Juice Cocktail, 208
    Better Belly, 207
    daily menus and, 218

Energy Enhancer, The, 210
Flu Away, 207
Glowing Skin Juice, 209
Healthy Heart Juice, 209
Mexican Delight, 210
Orange Dream Cycle, 211
Sweetie Pie, 208
Tropical Sunshine, 211

K
kale
    Hearty Chicken Vegetable Soup, *54*, 55
    Kale and Sweet Potato Salad, 82, 218, 219
kidney beans, in Vegetarian Chili, *140*, 141
Kulpinski, Tonijean, personal story, 19–23, 27–29

L
Lamb Soup, Siberian, 56, 218
lemon juice
    with water, 31
    Lentil Soup, Hearty Tri-Color, *48*, 49, 217, 219

M
maca powder
    Hawaiian Delight (smoothie), 213,
    My Daily Elixir (smoothie), 214
    Strawberry Oatmeal Maca Muffins, *156*, 157, 217, 219
    Vanilla Protein Power Smoothie, *212*, 213
Maker's Diet, The (Rubin), 20
Macaroni, Grandma Fran's Sicilian Baked, *118*, 119–120
mango
    Hawaiian Delight (juice), 213
    Tropical Sunshine (juice), 211

Mango and Watermelon Salad, *66*, 67, 220
Matthew Clark's Sweet, Crunchy, Delicious Salad, 79
meat
    from local sources, 26
    menu examples, 217–218
Mediterranean Arugula Salad with Heirloom Tomatoes, 86, 219
menus, daily, 217–221
Mexican Delight (juice), 210
Michelle's Black Bean Brownies, *192*, 193
Mouth-Watering Chicken Franchese, *134*, 135, 219
muffins
    Blueberry Muffins, 198
    Gluten-Free Blueberry Muffins, *40*, 41, 198, 219
    Strawberry Oatmeal Maca Muffins, *156*, 157, 217
mushrooms
    Cream of Mushroom Crock Pot Chicken, 124
    Creamy Kamut Pasta with Chicken and Broccoli, 121, 217
    Grandma Fran's *Pasta e Piselli*, *126*, 127
    Grandma Fran's Stuffed Mushrooms, *104*, 105
    shitake, and Healing Mineral Soup, 58, 219
My Daily Elixir (smoothie), 214
My Family's Thanksgiving Stuffing, 110

N
Nature's Kountry Healthy Food Store, 21

O

oils, substitutes for hydrogenated oils, 59
Orange Dream Cycle (juice), 211
organic food
    budgeting for, 25–27
    defined, 23
    farmers' markets, 26
    ingredients, for recipes, 32
Oatmeal Cranberry Cookies, *186*, 187
Oatmeal, Tonijean's Hearty, 35

P

Pancakes
    Cinnamon Banana Walnut, *38*, 39, 219
    Einkorn Blueberry, 43, 217
    Fluffy Coconut Pancakes, 44, 219
pasta recipes
    Amazingly Delicious and Creamy Red Lentil Pasta Pesto, *138*, 139
    Creamy Kamut Pasta with Chicken and Broccoli, 121, 217
    Grandma Fran's Pasta e Piselli, *126*, 127
    Grandma Fran's Sicilian Baked Macaroni, *118*, 119–120
    High-Antioxidant Red Lentil Pasta, 148
    Italian Pomodoro with Pasta, *128*, 129, 218
    Pasta Che Non Basta, *142*, 143
    Pasta Bolognese, 125, 217, 218
    Raw Vegan Fettuccine Alfredo, *114*, 115
    Red Lentil Pasta Alfredo with Broccoli, *132*, 133
    Zucchini Pasta Italiano, *136*, 137
pear salad with arugula and feta, *84*, 85, 220
Pecorino Romano cheese
    Amazingly Delicious and Creamy Red Lentil Pasta Pesto, *138*, 139
    Grandma Fran's Sicilian Baked Macaroni, *118*, 119–120
    Homemade Meatballs, *116*, 117, 218
pesto
    Amazingly Delicious and Creamy Red Lentil Pasta Pesto, *138*, 139
    Grandma Fran's Pesto, *96*, 97
    Zucchini Noodles with Creamy Walnut Pesto, 149
Pizza, Cauliflower, *102*, 103
Popeye's Spinach Salad, *70*, 71, 219
Porridge Tri-Color Quinoa Breakfast, *36*, 37
portabella mushrooms
    Cauliflower Fried Rice, *130*, 131
    Cream of Mushroom Crock Pot Chicken, 124
potatoes. *See also* sweet potatoes
    Grandma Fran's String Bean Salad, 77, 219
    Potato Salad: Three Ways, *60*, 61, 219
    Siberian Lamb Soup, 56, 218
prayer, before meals, 223
protein. *See also* high-protein entries
    versus fiber, 16
    for vegetarians, 16

Q

Quinoa
    Hearty Tri-Color Lentil Soup, *48*, 49, 217, 219
    Hearty Vegetable Soup with Quinoa, 57, 217
    High-Protein Pasta Salad, 87, 218
    pasta, as side with soup, 218
    Salad with Chickpeas, *62*, 63
    Tri-Color, for Breakfast Porridge, *36*, 37, 219

Tri-Color Pilaf, 147
Vegetable Soup, Hearty, 57, 217, 219

R
raw foods
    Delicious Raw Granola Bars, 152
    Easy Raw Apricot Bars, 201
    raw cacao, 153
    Raw Cacao, Banana, Avocado Mousse in Three Easy Steps, *180*, 181
    Raw Cacao Fudge Truffles, 202
    RAWlicious Banana Fudge Recipe, 200
    Raw Magic Bars, *170*, 171
    Raw Rocky Road Fudge, *194*, 195
    Raw Vegan Fettuccine Alfredo, *114*, 115
    Toni's Easy and Healthy Trail Mix, 155
red lentil pasta
    Amazingly Delicious and Creamy Red Lentil Pasta Pesto, *138*, 139
    High-Antioxidant Red Lentil Pasta, 148
    red lentil pasta, 217
    Red Lentil Pasta Alfredo with Broccoli, *132*, 133
rice
    My Family's Thanksgiving Stuffing, 110
    rice pudding, *168*, 169
Rocky Road Ice Cream, Grandma Fran's, 191
Rubin, Jordan, *The Maker's Diet*, 21

S
salad dressing
    Creamy Ranch Dressing, *90*, 91
    High-Antioxidant Salad Dressing, 92
salads
    Arame Salad, *80*, 81
    Arugula and Pear Salad with Feta, *84*, 85, 220
    Beet Salad, *68*, 69
    Grandma Fran's String Bean Salad, 77, 219
    Grandma Fran's Wild Flounder Salad, 78, 218
    High-Energy Healing Salad, *64*, 65
    High-Enzymatic Salad, 89
    High-Protein Kale Salad, 87, 218
    High-Protein Pasta Salad, 88, 218
    Kale and Sweet Potato Salad, 82, 218, 219
    Mango and Watermelon Salad, *66*, 67, 219
    Matthew Clark's Sweet, Crunchy, Delicious Salad, 79
    Mediterranean Arugula Salad with Heirloom Tomatoes, 86, 219
    Popeye's Spinach Salad, *70*, 71, 219
    Potato Salad: Three Ways, *60*, 61, 219
    Quinoa Salad with Chickpeas, *62*, 63
    Red Cabbage Salad, *74*, 75, 220
    Sweetest Potato Salad, The, *72*, 73
    Warm Arame Salad, 82
    What's in the Fridge Salad, 83, 219
sauerkraut, 89, 113, 217, 218
seaweed
    Arame Salad, *80*, 81
    Warm Arame Salad, 82
Siberian Lamb Soup, 56, 218
Sicilian Baked Macaroni, Grandma Fran's, *118*, 119–120
salt, tips about, 42, 203
smoothies. *See also* juices
    Amazingly Delicious Raw Fudge Banana Split Smoothie, 214
    Hawaiian Delight, 213
    My Daily Elixir, 214

    Vanilla Protein Power Smoothie, *212*, 213
snacks
    Delicious Raw Granola Bars, 152
    health tip about, 221
    High-Protein Nourishing Snack, 158
    Strawberry Oatmeal Maca Muffins, *156*, 157, 217, 219
    Toni's Easy and Healthy Trail Mix, 155, 217
soups
    Creamy Butternut Squash Soup, *50*, 51, 220
    Delicious Creamy Sweet Potato Soup, 53, 220
    Healing Mineral Soup, 58
    Hearty Chicken Vegetable Soup, *54*, 55, 218
    Hearty Tri-Color Lentil Soup, *48*, 49, 217, 219
    Hearty Vegetable Soup with Quinoa, 57, 217
    pumpkin soup, *52*
    sweet potato soup, *52*, 53, 220
    Siberian Lamb Soup, 56, 218
Spinach Salad, *70*, 71, 219
Standard American Diet (SAD), 16
Strawberry Oatmeal Maca Muffins, *156*, 157, 217, 219
String Bean Salad, Grandma Fran's, 77, 219
Stuffing, My Family's Thanksgiving, 110
sugars, kinds of, 16
Sweetie Pie (juice), 208
sweet potatoes
    Delicious, Creamy Sweet Potato Soup, 53, 219
    Hearty Chicken Vegetable Soup, *54*, 55
    Hearty Vegetable Soup with Quinoa, 57, 217
    Kale and Sweet Potato Salad, 82, 218, 219
    Sweet Potato Soup, *52*, 53, 220
    Vegetarian Thai Cuisine in Seven Easy Steps, 144, 219

T

Thai Cuisine in Seven Easy Steps, Vegetarian, 144–145, 219
tomatoes. *See also* cherry tomatoes
    Grandma Fran's Bruschetta, *94*, 95
    Hearty Vegetable Soup with Quinoa, 57, 217
    Italian Pomodoro with Pasta, *128*, 129, 218
    Mediterranean Arugula Salad with Heirloom Tomatoes, 86, 219
    Pasta Che Non Basta, *142*, 143
    Siberian Lamb Soup, 56, 218
    Vegetarian Chili, *140*, 141
Tonijean's Hearty Oatmeal, *34*, 35, 219
Toni's Delicious Banana Walnut Bread, *162*, 163
Toni's Easy and Healthy Trail Mix, 155, 217
Tri-Color Quinoa Breakfast Porridge, *36*, 37
Tri-Color Quinoa Pilaf, 147
Tropical Sunshine (juice), 211

V

vacation time, six suggestions for meals, 203–205
Vanilla Protein Power Smoothie, *212*, 213
vegan recipes
    Raw Vegan Fettucine Alfredo, *114*, 115
Vegetable Soup with Quinoa, Hearty, 57, 217
vegetarian recipes

Creamy Butternut Squash Soup, *50*, 51, 220

Healing Mineral Soup, 58

Hearty Vegetable Soup with Quinoa, 57, 217

menus, samples of, 219

Sweet Potato Soup, Delicious Creamy, 53, 220

Vegetarian Chili, *140*, 141

Vegetarian Thai Cuisine in Seven Easy Steps, 144–145, 219

W

Walnut Pesto with Zucchini Noodles, 149

Warm Arame Salad, 83

water
  before breakfast, 31
  health tips about, 157, 212

Watermelon and Mango Salad, *66*, 67, 219

Wild Alaskan Sockeye Salmon Teriyaki, *112*, 113, 218

Wild Flounder Salad, Grandma Fran's, 78, 218

Z

zucchini
  Grandma Fran's Italian Style Zucchini, 146
  Raw Vegan Fettuccine Alfredo, *114*, 115
  Vegetarian Thai Cuisine in Seven Easy Steps, 144
  Zucchini Noodles with Creamy Walnut Pesto, 149
  Zucchini Pasta Italiano, *136*, 137

About the Author

Tonijean Kulpinski is a board certified Holistic, Drugless Practitioner, a Certified Biblical Health Coach, and a member of The American Association of Drugless Practitioners and The Weston A. Price Foundation. She is a graduate of The Institute for Integrative Nutrition, the world's largest nutrition school.

Tonijean is the best-selling author of the book entitled, *Stop Battling Disease & Start Building Wellness: Your Guide to Extraordinary Health*. She is the owner of Heaven on Earth Healing Center, Inc., where she educates patients how to stop battling disease and start building wellness every day.

Tonijean has made several television appearances on Trinity Broadcast Network (TBN): *Joy in Our Town*, and *Doctor to Doctor*, televised from The Manhattan Studio. She has also appeared on *The Victorious Life Show* with Lisa Buldo and *Book Talk* with Bill Lamanski.

She bases her teachings on raw, whole, organic superfood nutrition and the principles that are stated clearly in scripture. She believes in eating food in the form God created as it is the medicine that truly heals. Tonijean gives holistic nutrition seminars around the country where she shares these principles.

Tonijean lives with her wonderful husband, Vladimir, their precious daughter, Michaela, and their loving golden retriever, Peanut.

Made in the USA
Middletown, DE
01 May 2019